"This biography reveals that there are ordinary men who become extraordinary by dint of parental influence and patience, near-limitless curiosity, a desire to learn more, and a desire to see more places. The author was driven by a consuming desire to tell people about what fires the determination and spirit of such a man for an entire lifetime."

—from Foreword by Lynn A. Greenwalt,
former director of the US Fish and Wildlife Service

"Gifted with a naturalist's heart, an artist's eye, and a deft hand with pencil, pen, or paintbrush, Bob Hines spent more than half a century creating the images through which millions of Americans learned about their natural heritage. *Bob Hines: National Wildlife Artist* restores this seminal artist to the ranks of the greats, where he belongs."

—Scott Weidensaul, author of *Of a Feather: A Brief History of American Birding*
and *The First Frontier: The Forgotten History of Struggle, Savagery, and Endurance in Early America*

"This biography tells the often sad but ultimately triumphant story of the man who painted dozens of masterpieces, recounting the role of the US Fish and Wildlife Service as a key patron of the arts in promoting wildlife conservation through Hines's exceptional artwork."

—Dyana Furmansky, author of *Rosalie Edge, Hawk of Mercy*

"From Boy Scout to master artist, Bob Hines never varied from excellence. He achieved with pen and brush what Ansel Adams achieved with a camera. No wildlife artist has ever been able to duplicate Hines's level of perfection in animal artistry."

—Cecil D. Andrus, former secretary of the Department of the Interior

"Bob Hines was a superb artist who captured the beauty of wildlife in their natural habitats and wildlife scenes that fascinate all lovers of wildlife.... I am delighted by John Juriga's history of Bob Hines, the renowned wildlife artist who was an important member of the US Fish and Wildlife Service. His work brought acclaim and furthered the cause of wise wildlife conservation."

—Nathaniel Reed, former assistant secretary of the Department of the Interior

Bob Hines

Under Ohio Skies

As Told by The Conservation Division

Bob Hines

NATIONAL WILDLIFE ARTIST

John D. Juriga

Foreword by Lynn A. Greenwalt

ISBN: 978-1-59298-440-4
Library of Congress Control Number: 2011963246

Cover photo of Bob Hines used with permission
from the Ohio Department of Natural Resources.
Cover image of killdeer courtesy of the US Fish and Wildlife Service.
Under Ohio Skies and *The Ohio Conservation Bulletin* panels reproduced with permission from the Ohio Department of Natural Resources. Mallard drake drawing on chapter 6 courtesy of David McBride. Other Bob Hines clip art at chapter headings courtesy of the US Fish and Wildlife Service.

Book design by Ryan Scheife, Mayfly Design
Printed in the United States of America
Printed on recycled paper
First Printing: 2012

16 15 14 13 12 5 4 3 2 1

Beaver's Pond Press, Inc.
7108 Ohms Lane, Edina, MN 55439-2129
(952) 829-8818 • www.BeaversPondPress.com

To order, visit www.BeaversPondBooks.com or call (800) 901-3480. Reseller discounts available.

Dedication

For my wife, Frances Biller Juriga—After nearly twenty-five years of marriage, your beauty and grace, wisdom and strength continue to inspire me. With heartfelt appreciation of your love and support.

~J.D.J.

Bob's precise knowledge of the anatomy of birds, fish, and mammals came from practical experience with specimens at hand and with extensive observation in the field. His crisp pen drawings show mastery of that technique.... Drawing often for the professionals, he passed their standards for accuracy of anatomy and lifelike poses, thus also appealing to the general public who could sense the veracity of his work without knowing the details.

~Shirley A. Briggs. "Rachel Carson Council News." December 1994. No. 84:3.

Contents

Foreword

I had known Bob Hines in a casual way for several years when I was named director of the US Fish and Wildlife Service, and in that role I came to more fully understand what it meant to have a National Wildlife Artist as an employee. I was much younger then, and I was only beginning to realize that even the most ordinary-seeming people may have responded to life, its uncertainties and opportunities in ways that resulted in the formation of a truly remarkable person. Bob Hines—small of stature, cheerful in outlook, and without any pretense whatsoever—was at first glance a most ordinary man.

After I had been director for a time, I began to make fairly frequent trips up to the north penthouse of the massive Department of the Interior building where Bob had his cluttered studio and peace and quiet prevailed. I knew I would be greeted with his hail of "Hello, director! Come in and sit down." Bob was always happy to show me what he was doing, some of the details of a painting or the nuances of line and shadow in a pencil sketch, and to make small talk. It was a place for respite and recovery, where phones seldom rang and I could spend a few minutes in the company of a gentle man who knew how to take my mind off the pressures present two floors down in a corner office. I have a feeling I may not have been the first director to take refuge in that small office for a few moments, and I began to believe there was more to Bob Hines than an obvious talent for illustration.

Bob's reputation as an artist was well known; with the help of his remarkable secretary, Bea Boone, their management of the complex process of choosing the illustration for the annual Federal Migratory Bird Hunting stamp, the famous Duck Stamp, was evident to all who observed it. His illustrations added information to countless brochures and publications, and even provoked keen interest from members of Congress, who found Bob's pen-and-ink sketches blessed relief from the staid and bureaucratic language and charts of many an annual budget document.

His talent was formidable and his work legendary for its accuracy and attention to the details that make the difference between the merely interesting and the truly impressive. It was work that complemented the writing of Rachel Carson, whose books on natural history were widely read and some amply illustrated with Hines's work. He had polished his own talent for writing years before, producing news items and other material for sportsmen's publications and state fish and game materials. His artwork and the accurate information that went with them were popular and widely respected.

I am convinced that only his closest friends and colleagues knew much at all about the otherwise ordinary man. I knew almost nothing about his life and early activity. After I saw him for the last time at his retirement send-off in 1981, I feared that neither I nor anyone else would ever know the full story of the life of this unusual human being. There might never be a record of what forces and events created this man who became a treasure in his own right and certainly worthy of being called the National Wildlife Artist.

John Juriga, whom I met by virtue of my owning a Hines painting, revealed a boundless enthusiasm for Hines and his work. With characteristic gentle persistence, John persuaded me to help him get Hines the kind of recognition he deserved. Out of Juriga's effort has come this biography which reveals that there are ordinary men who become extraordinary by dint of parental influence and patience, near-limitless curiosity, a desire to learn more, and a desire to see more places. The author was driven by a consuming desire to tell people about what fires the determination and spirit of such a man for an entire lifetime.

This book reinforces the truism that one should never judge a person by what he seems to be, because in almost every case that judgment will fall short of the mark. This is especially true of Hines, whose life is worth examining so that others can be impressed and perhaps inspired by a story about a heroic American. He lived a life of adventure and notable accomplishment, without fanfare and little fame. That life was driven by "the mind of a sage and the soul of a boy"—the man who lived it plied his trade in a way that moved and informed and inspired millions, yet has remained largely unknown. Until now.

~Lynn A. Greenwalt
Derwood, Maryland
November 23, 2011

Acknowledgments

Few figures were more emblematic of the National Wildlife Refuge System than Bob Hines, the singular National Wildlife Artist for the US Fish and Wildlife Service (US FWS). To celebrate the centennial of the National Wildlife Refuge system in 2003, the Ward Museum of Wildfowl Art in Salisbury, Maryland, hosted a major exhibit, "Bob Hines: National Wildlife Artist." As guest curator for this first retrospective of Hines's career, I compiled a narrative of his life and accomplishments. I recall discovering such new information about Hines that deserved a more detailed treatment. One of the highlights of the Ward event was meeting Thomas O. Duncan at the opening reception. A fisheries biologist by training, Tom was a contemporary of Hines, who conceived the notion of a Hines biography. As the centennial of Hines's birth approached on the horizon, in a moment of weakness, I accepted the baton to author a book on Hines. Tom has remained a trusted member of my Bob Hines "think tank."

I embarked on the Hines biography with a considerable degree of naiveté. My original intent was to conduct the research myself during my leisure. However, I quickly learned that it takes a village to flesh out the details of a person's life. This project could not proceed without the support of Frances Biller Juriga, my beloved wife, who has shared our marriage with Bob Hines intermittently over the past decade. As I began to write my first chapter drafts she pleasantly surprised me with her keen instincts as an editor and proofreader. Fran remains steadfastly as determined to see this completed volume of the Hines biography as I am. For that reason and countless others I affectionately dedicate this book to her.

I am indebted to Beaver's Pond Press (BPP) for its willingness to publish this biography of Hines. After a disappointing string of rejections, Jordan Wiklund, an acquisitions editor for BPP, granted me a first taste of interest and enthusiasm regarding my manuscript. April Michelle Davis tightened my writing with her editorial expertise. Amy Quale of BPP patiently mentored me through the publishing process. Ryan Scheife of Mayfly Design met the design challenges for this book, beautifully complementing both the text and the illustrations. By happenstance, Ryan had had eight framed Bob Hines bird prints displayed in his home well before he agreed to this assignment. I am confident that wildlife artist Hines would appreciate the nature thread of Beaver's Pond Press, Mayfly Design, and the fact that the editor of his biography is a Quale.

I want to thank Executive Director Lora Bottinelli and the curatorial committee of the Ward Museum of Wildfowl Art for their trust in me as I assembled the Hines art exhibit in 2003. I was unprepared for the generosity of Russell Fink of Lorton, Virginia, for materials displayed during the Ward event. Russ purchased the Hines estate following Bob's death in 1994. I shudder to think how lacking the Ward exhibit and this biography would have been without the items from Russ's collection. That initial collaboration evolved into a welcome friendship with Russ and his lovely wife Marlee, both of whom have stood behind me as my efforts segued toward a biography of Hines and the restaging of an art exhibit during the Hines centennial year. Many of the color plates in this volume are reproductions of Russ's detailed transparencies that he used to catalog the Hines estate.

Nancy Hines, Bob's daughter, gave me her blessing to research her father's life. I truly appreciate her confidence in me. Another special relative, NH, requested complete anonymity. However, her contributions were so important that I could not in good conscience omit NH from my acknowledgments.

Dr. Mark Madison, historian at the US FWS National Conservation and Training Center, Shepherdstown, West Virginia, encouraged me at every step since my initial inquiry about Hines nearly a decade ago. I can count on his infectious enthusiasm without fail. A wealth of information exists in a 1991 oral history with Hines and Pete Anastasi. Mark kindly provided me a copy of the written transcript from this interview courtesy of the NCTC archives. Mark Madison, along with Mark Newcastle, also with the USFWS, facilitated many of the images that appear on these pages. Jeanne Harold and David Klinger at NCTC likewise have agreed with my efforts to reveal Hines's accomplishments to a contemporary audience. Anne Roy, of the NCTC library, located several obscure references for me.

Three individuals have acted as my research associates. Kathleen Marine, genealogist extraordinaire, uncovered many hidden facts regarding the Hines family in Ohio. Without her efforts, Nathan Hines (Bob's paternal grandfather) and his imprisonment during the American Civil War might be lost to history. Kathleen's willingness to dig deeper for details energized my personal quest to continue this project to completion despite an occasional speed bump. I now know more about the Hines family ancestry than I do my own. John Ullrich cheerfully combed through the Houghton Mifflin archives at Harvard University's Houghton Library, thereby directing me when I later accessed the Rachel Carson Papers at Yale University's Beinecke Rare Book and Manuscript Library. Allison Badger patiently browsed through the Outdoor Writers Association of America archives at Mansfield Library, University of Montana in Missoula. Like a prospector panning for gold, Allison discovered an occasional well-worded nugget referring to Hines as a member of that organization.

Murray Hines graciously responded to my request for additional information on the Hines family. With a few computer keystrokes and mouse clicks, he readily shared his results of untold hours of research into the John and Mary Roderick Hines family genealogy. Anyone whose research includes Rachel Carson owes a debt of gratitude to Linda Lear, author of the splendid biography *Rachel Carson: Witness for Nature*. Lear's painstaking research of Carson's life has provided invaluable sources of reference for future Carson scholars. I thank Dr. Lear for her words of advice with this Hines project. Dr. Barbara Ward Klein challenged me to articulate better my interest in Hines to entice readers of this book. My one wish is that I have succeeded in that particular goal. William Webster shared with me an unexpected gem—a copy of Hines's 1933 journal that reveals his uncertainty and despair during that year of the Great Depression.

I especially want to thank Pete Anastasi, Hines's trusted colleague and personal friend, and Pete's wife Betty, who welcomed me into their beautiful home in Manassas, Virginia. Pete spent the better part of an afternoon sitting in the hot seat while answering my rapid-fire questions. Several other individuals shared their memories of Hines with me: Cecil Andrus, Ray Arnett, Debra Berke, Bobbie Hines Blowers, Grayson Chesser, Frank Cockrell, Delbert "Cigar" Daisey, Dial Dunkin, Russell Fink, Nancy Hines, NH, Robert Glotzhober, Edith Gottschalk, Lynn Greenwalt, Clay Hardy, Jo Keller, Jim Marshall, Jim McGrady, Tim Miller, Phil Million, Jim Palmer, Don Pfitzer, Christine and Bill Raffalt, Nathaniel Reed, George Reiger, V. Daniel Stiles, Elsa Thompson, and George Watson. David McBride, author of *The Federal Duck Stamps: A Complete Guide* (Winchester Press, 1984) encouraged me with this project and graciously shared his Hines drawing of a rising mallard drake that graces the frontispiece of McBride's book.

The Steele Memorial Library in Elmira, New York, deserves special recognition for its reference librarians' unflinching demeanor despite my multiple requests for interlibrary loans. I discovered a new ally in the library of the American Philatelic Society, Bellefonte, Pennsylvania. Ellen Peachy, a former member of the library staff there, located the specific reference that includes Hines's 1957 whooping crane design as one of the ten best stamps in the world for that year.

The Columbus Dispatch granted me permission to excerpt Hines's series of newspaper articles printed after his Alaskan trek in 1947. The Ohio Department of Natural Resources permits me to reproduce Hines's materials from *The Ohio Conservation Bulletin*. Eileen Terrill, managing editor for *Yankee*, approved my request to quote passages from Hines's 1991 magazine article, "Remembering Rachel." Sarah Yake of the Frances Collin Literary Agency facilitated my inquiry to quote from Rachel Carson's correspondence. Excerpts from the unpublished Carson materials are copyright 2011 by Roger A. Christie; reprinted by permission of Frances Collin, Trustee.

I want to thank the Rutherford B. Hayes Presidential Center in Fremont, Ohio, for their willingness to host the Bob Hines centennial exhibit. I appreciate the warm welcome the executive director, Tom Culbertson, and curator Nan Card extended to my wife and me during our initial visit to the Hayes Center. There is special significance in having the Hines exhibit in Fremont, a homecoming of sorts as Fremont was the site of Hines's boyhood.

I have a personal obligation to acknowledge a few more individuals who contributed to this project. My mother, Mary Juriga, who at the time of this writing is a respectable ninety-three years of age, still maintains a sincere interest in the well-being of others. I thank her not only for her gift of unconditional love, but also for her social nature that subliminally directed me to appreciate the genre of biography and memoir. Two special couples provided hospitality to me during my research travels—Mary and Tom Karazsia, and Valerie and Wayne Bushey. The former are family members who are friends, the latter are friends who have become family members. I also want to thank my good friend Dr. Bryan Karazsia, who just happens to be my nephew. Bryan assisted his technologically challenged uncle by converting my chapter drafts into unalterable PDFs. He also rescued me by returning my Word documents after my computer suddenly died, stealing my entire manuscript.

The Association of Retired Fish and Wildlife Service Employees is a cohesive group whose passion for wildlife and the outdoors remains undiminished. During the autumn of 2009 the retirees invited me to speak about Hines at their annual reunion held that year in Kennebunkport, Maine. The Heritage Committee of the Service presented me its Heritage Award in part because of my scholarship on Bob Hines. I had the opportunity to meet Sam Hamilton, the newly appointed director of the US FWS. Mr. Hamilton rose through the ranks of the organization to become regional director of the southeast region of the US FWS before his promotion to full director. Like many others, I was shocked to learn that four months after meeting Mr. Hamilton he died suddenly at fifty-four years of age while skiing in Colorado. It is my sincere hope that Hamilton's balanced vision of a realistic approach to future environmental challenges based on sound scientific data will be his lasting legacy.

In closing, I want to salute the members of the US FWS—past, present, and future—along with those of other federal, state, and grassroots conservation organizations as advocates for the integrity of the natural world that sustains all life on earth. When Rachel Carson accepted the Audubon Society Medal in 1963 following the release of *Silent Spring* she wisely remarked, "The goal of conservation has no end. There is no point where we can say, 'Our work is finished.'"

Introduction

History seldom occurs in the moment. Often it develops imperceptibly as future generations gain a new perspective of past events through the refractive lens of time. It seems fitting that Bob Hines hailed from Ohio, which has played a crucial role in US history. If the Buckeye State contributed no fewer than eight US presidents, why should it not yield one of the premier wildlife artists of the twentieth century? The story of Hines's life and works is not about fame or fortune; rather it is one of talent and perseverance. He was a common man with uncommon artistic gifts. An examination of his accomplishments gives one a glimpse into the history of conservation efforts during the last century.

Ohio became a crucible for Bob Hines's personal maturation and professional growth. While a youngster, he turned to drawing as a means to comfort his mother, bereft over the loss of her newborn daughter. After his beloved mother died, Hines sublimated his grief with the companionship of animals in a backyard menagerie. His immersion in the Boy Scouts further encouraged his fascination with the richness of Ohio's natural beauty. Hines's high school yearbook presciently describes him as having "[t]he mind of a sage, and the soul of a boy." During the darkness and despair of the Great Depression, Hines found his calling—he returned to drawing in an effort to enlighten and inform the public about Ohio's wildlife. Untrained and uneducated, Hines began his career with the Ohio Division of Conservation and Natural Resources. His work there sowed the seeds of environmental awareness a full generation before it penetrated the public consciousness. He fulfilled his goal of designing a Federal Duck Stamp. It was inevitable that Hines's sphere of influence would expand beyond the borders of his home state of Ohio to include the goals of conservation throughout the United States and abroad through his work with the US Fish and Wildlife Service (US FWS). When Hines joined the Service, his first supervisor was Rachel Carson, a little known biologist who later became an icon of the modern environmental movement. Carson asked Hines to illustrate her third book, *The Edge of the Sea.* Their collaboration became the intersection of two remarkable talents. As a federal employee, Hines changed the format of the selection process for the annual Duck Stamp to an open competition, thereby elevating the event to achieve national prominence. He managed the judging of the Duck Stamp competition for over thirty years. Hines also designed the first four wildlife conservation postage stamps that introduced the term *conservation* to the general public during the mid-1950s, a decade before the word entered the national lexicon.

Lynn Greenwalt, former director of the US FWS, described Hines as a "mysterious fixture" at the organization. Indeed Hines's life was one of contradictions. He interfaced with the leading experts in wildlife biology, yet as a self-taught artist, he had no further education beyond high school. His career benefited from influential mentors, yet he was an absent parent to his own children during their formative years. He coordinated the Federal Duck Stamp contest that afforded the winning designers financial gain, though as a federal employee living on a modest income he himself could not participate in the competition as an artist. Though Hines's artwork received wide distribution in the public domain, his reputation as an artist has been unappreciated because of its rarity in the commercial market. Hines held a unique niche within the US FWS. He felt a special calling because of his artistic contributions. Some career bureaucrats at the Interior Department incorrectly interpreted his sense of mission as arrogance, an exaggerated sense of self-importance.

Bob Hines's life demonstrates what someone can contribute with no formal art or academic training, but with innate talent and confidence in his abilities. When we describe conservationists, we usually think in terms of scientists, writers, or activists. However, Hines used his artistic talents to create a visual imprint that helped promote the various US FWS endeavors in those seminal early decades. Moreover, his dedication to elevating the standards of the Federal Duck Stamp competition ultimately generated millions of dollars of revenue for waterfowl habitat preservation and restoration while promoting the genre of wildlife art.

In the early stages of my research, I came to a delightful conclusion: the more I learned about Hines, the more I liked him as a person. Aside from true talent, he had a generous spirit and a friendly demeanor. The more I liked him, the more I felt he deserved recognition. Now as the centennial of Bob Hines's birth approaches, with that refractive lens of history, I wish to examine his legacy in the art of conservation. As the United States' singular National Wildlife Artist, Hines created an impressive visual legacy that persists in private collections, refuges, and visitors' centers. It would be a great disservice to future generations if Hines's life story and accomplishments faded into obscurity.

~John D. Juriga
October 2011

Chapter One

The Mind of a Sage and the Soul of a Boy

A genealogy of the Hines family reveals a common bond with the state of Ohio that embraces five generations. The roots of the Hines family tree are shrouded in mystery but may have their origin in the Palatinate region of Germany. During the great exodus of Palatine Germans around 1709, an ancestral Hines member may have emigrated from his homeland to Ireland by way of London. At the open invitation of William Penn, this forbear likely arrived in America then migrated westward with other German émigrés. The first documented milestone in the Hines family was the 1795 marriage in Frederick County, Maryland, between John Hines and Mary Roderick. The newlyweds settled in nearby Hampshire County, Virginia, where they became parents of nine children including a son, Nathaniel, their sixth child, born in 1808. (Decades later, this area became incorporated into the Eastern Panhandle of West Virginia after it seceded from Virginia in 1863.) John Hines along with his family appears in the 1810 county census. John reportedly died of an accidental gunshot injury around 1815 as his name is absent in the subsequent 1820 census. Shortly thereafter, Mary Roderick Hines moved her children farther west to Coshocton County, Ohio, where they joined other members of the extended Hines and Roderick families.

In 1830, Nathaniel Hines married Delilah Brelsford, who likewise migrated from Hampshire County, Virginia, to Ohio. Their union yielded seven children; Nathaniel ("Nathan") Warren Hines, the youngest child, was born in 1841. The Hines family relocated to Peoria, Illinois, for a brief sojourn of six months during which the elder Hines likely joined his brother. However, Nathaniel and Delilah, along with their children, returned to Ohio where they settled on the St. Clair farm among the gently rolling hills of Muskingum County. Nathaniel became very involved in local government, having faithfully served as a justice of the peace for several years.

As the Civil War escalated, twenty-one-year-old Nathan Hines enlisted for a three-year commitment as a private in the Union Army with the 122nd Infantry Regiment of Ohio. Initially with 927 men, the infantry departed Ohio then encamped in Parkersburg, West Virginia, prior to entering Virginia. For several months, the men engaged in garrison and guard duties. Pressing onward with other companies, they became involved in several skirmishes before they broke through the Confederate lines and marched into Harper's Ferry, West Virginia. The fighting intensified as the men joined in the Fight of the Wilderness, losing over 120 soldiers on the first day of that conflict. The troops traveled farther into Virginia, crossed the Appomattox, then appropriated a key railroad around Petersburg. During the Battle of Cold Harbor in June 1864, the Confederate troops captured Nathan Hines, sending him to the Andersonville Prison in Georgia. Hines's death notice states: "Few of the younger generation are acquainted with the horrors inflicted upon the Union soldiers who were imprisoned at Andersonville. It is regarded as the most cruel prison this country has ever seen." Indeed the odds of dying in the prison were considerable—nearly one-third of the prisoners succumbed to the triad of malnutrition, overcrowding, and disease. Hines spent eleven months "in the famous rebel prison," then was released in April 1865 before his official discharge from military service the following month. Because of his imprisonment, Nathan Hines missed the opportunity to rejoin his fellow members of the 122nd Ohio Regiment as they witnessed Robert E. Lee's surrender at Appomattox, Virginia, earlier that April.

Returning to civilian life, Nathan worked on the family farm as a laborer. In 1866, he wed Nancy Madden, a resident of nearby New Concord, Ohio; that marriage yielded four children. After Nathan's aged parents retired from farming, he began working for the B&O Railroad as an agent at the New Concord office in 1875. By 1880, when Nathan accepted a transfer with the railroad, he along with his family left central Ohio for Sandusky, a city of 15,800 in Erie County perched on the shores of Lake Erie. Upon their arrival, Nancy Madden Hines gave birth to another son, George Warren Hines, in 1881. The Sandusky city directory for 1886 lists Nathan Hines as an agent for the Baltimore and Ohio Express rail line. Nancy Hines appears as head waitress for the West House; she later became the proprietress of the Waldorf boarding house. A few lines in the local paper reveal that Mr. N. W. Hines departed for his former home of Zanesville, Ohio, in 1891 to celebrate his twenty-fifth wedding anniversary (presumably his wife accompanied him). The following year, Nathan changed employers joining the People's Electric Railroad. Son George ended his formal education after eight years of schooling to assist his mother at the boarding house.

In August 1900, the family experienced a tragic event that threatened its security. Nathan Hines had found employment as an operator of a trolley for the Sandusky, Milan & Norwalk Electric Railroad Company. Early on the morning of August 28, Hines was returning from Milan with a load of empty beer kegs and cases. At the same time, a B&O locomotive with seven cars, some loaded with coal, was backing into a depot. As Hines approached a crossing, he disengaged his electric power and applied the brakes. The rails, wet with dew, allowed the vehicle to slide forward on the tracks even though the wheels were not turning. Hines then attempted to reverse his direction, but the momentum of the trolley propelled it farther, colliding with the locomotive cab. There was a tumult of tumbling beer bottles and kegs that pinned Hines in a narrow space. Miraculously, he was unscathed despite a corner of the trolley having been torn away from the force of the collision.

Frank Seeber, engineer of the larger locomotive, was not so fortunate. The force of the collision hurled him against the control panel, "his skull being crushed in, his jaw broken, left arm mangled, and other wounds inflicted." Seeber had been an employee of the railroad for ten years and an engineer for the past three. When he died at the scene, he was thirty-two years old and left a widow and a two-year-old child. The newspaper account of the accident describes Hines as being "almost prostrated" the morning of the accident. Other witnesses disagreed on their estimate of the trolley's speed prior to the collision. The acting coroner concluded that "said collision was caused by criminal carelessness on the part of Motorman Nathan

W. Hines." One month after the accident, as Nathan was returning from his evening route, the local sheriff served him an indictment for manslaughter, setting bond at $1,000. The trial began about six weeks later. After three days of testimony, the jury of "twelve wise men" found Hines not guilty of the manslaughter charge.

The stress of the trial exacted psychological as well as financial tolls on the family. To compound matters, there was widespread economic uncertainty as these early recession years of the new century were but a prelude to the Great Panic of 1907. Nancy Hines watched revenues decline from her boardinghouse with a liability of $1,200, approximating the bond amount set at the time of her husband's indictment. By February 1901, the local newspaper reporting Nancy's financial dilemma suggested that "sickness in the Hines family and the fact that certain boarders supposed to be trustworthy left suddenly without settling their accounts precipitated the assignment. In many respects the Waldorf has been a popular and successful establishment, but an unfortunate combination of circumstances forces the proprietress to the wall." Nancy had no other option than to sign over the facility with its assets of furniture and personal property of $2,000 to her creditors.

Son George Hines had relocated to Columbus. By September 1901, Nathan and Nancy Hines likewise moved to the state capital. Perhaps they wished to escape the notoriety of Nathan's trial and the public humiliation of Nancy's debt. Arriving in Columbus, Nathan and Nancy Hines parted emotionally if not physically. There is no evidence that Nathan was gainfully employed after the family left Sandusky. A photograph of Nathan Hines shows a distinguished, bearded gentleman with a long face. He is attired with a bow tie and suit coat of that era. His prominent ears appear to be a trait his grandsons inherited. Nathan's death notice provides details about his imprisonment at Andersonville, stating, "This terrible experience affected his health throughout his entire afterlife. His death was due to a gradual breaking down of the system." Curiously, the write-up includes the notation that Hines "carried a large life insurance." Nathan lived on his Civil War pension until he died of rheumatic heart disease at age sixty-six in June 1907 with his final address being his daughter's home in Magnetic Springs, Ohio.

George Hines's name appears for the first time in the 1906 Columbus city directory listed with a clerical occupation and a boarding address. On

September 10, 1907, he married Mabel Elwood Nunemacher. Mabel was born in Harrisburg, Pennsylvania, on March 26, 1885. Her parents, Harry Atmore and Katherine Barnitz Nunemacher, were born and reared in central Pennsylvania. Harry held a clerical position with the railroad, which required frequent relocations. In 1883 their son, George Nunemacher, was born in Round Rock, Texas. Shortly thereafter, the Nunemachers returned to central Pennsylvania for the birth of their daughter. When Mabel was a toddler, the family moved to Columbus, Ohio. Harry Nunemacher held a variety of clerical positions before he partnered with his wife's relative to open a successful jewelry store in the Columbus area. Aside from having a cleft palate, which may have given a nasal tone to her speech, there is little information on Mabel's childhood. Except for long walks together along the Scioto River, the details of Mabel's courtship with George Hines are likewise lost to history. George signed the marriage record in agreement "[t]hat neither of said parties is an habitual drunkard, epileptic, imbecile or insane, and is not under the influence of any intoxicating liquor or narcotic drug." Reverend Ramsey officiated the marriage ceremony. The marriage certificate for George and Mabel Hines states George as a salesman. For the next decade, he became a buyer of "wholesale notions" for the Tracy Wells Company, which distributed general merchandise.

George and Mabel Hines became parents with the birth of their son, William Atmore Hines, in 1909. A second son, Robert Warren Hines, was born February 6, 1912, although the local newspaper incorrectly lists his date of birth as February 10 in its list of birth announcements. George's mother, Nancy Madden Hines, also shared her son's address at the time of her death at seventy-three years of age from an intestinal malignancy in October 1915. Mabel eagerly anticipated having a daughter, but a blood type discrepancy complicated a subsequent pregnancy. Her third child, Mary Ann Hines, lived at the very most one day in August 1916. She may have been a premature newborn as her stated cause of death is "inanition." The death of Mary Ann Hines was a pivotal moment for the family. Mabel sank into a deep depression, forming a special emotional bond with her younger son. She became so bereft with the loss of her daughter that she dressed Bob in girl's clothing. George refused to consider fathering other children; he could not risk having his dear wife endure that sense of loss again. A devotee of nature, Mabel assuaged her grief on long walks in the outdoors with her son.

Young Bob Hines displayed an interest in drawing around age four, according to the collective memory of his family members. He started to draw pictures as a means to comfort his mother while she struggled with depression following the death of her newborn daughter. There were no other close relatives who displayed a talent for art. Bob inherited his facial features, especially his deeply set eyes, from his mother. A photograph of a young Mabel Nunemacher bears a strong resemblance to Bob's boyhood appearance. While living in Columbus, Bob followed in his brother's footsteps and attended Clintonville Elementary School. Mabel and George Hines encouraged their younger son's interest in animals. This boyhood fascination became the foundation for Bob's lifelong passion for nature and the out-of-doors. Bob fondly recalled their pet Airedale, named Nick: "He was quite the champion fighter on the street after he grew up.... [T]here were two bulldogs that bullied him, and I can remember the glorious feeling I had the day he whipped both of them at the same time."

By 1920, George Hines joined the North American Life Insurance Company as a general agent. The following year, he accepted a transfer to the Fremont office of the same company, moving his family with him. At that time, Fremont, the seat of Sandusky County, was a bustling town with a population around 12,500, surrounded by a patchwork of farm fields and pastures. Fremont had transitioned from a shipping center on the Sandusky River to more of a railroad-driven commerce. It achieved a historical footnote as being the final home of former President Rutherford B. Hayes and the site of the Hayes Presidential Library. With this relocation, George returned to the northwest corner of Ohio, closer to his childhood home of Sandusky. Bob's father had given him a diamondback terrapin, but the reptile did not survive the move to Fremont. Bob came of age on the level lands that flank the Sandusky River before it flows another sixteen miles to empty into Lake Erie at Sandusky Bay.

After the Hines family arrived in Fremont, father George changed careers to work in the Herbrand Company, a drop forge plant that manufactured tools and automotive parts. The family occupied a modest square wooden-framed house on Napoleon Street. Young Bob wandered barefoot on the park-like grounds of the Hayes Presidential Library until the burs of an American chestnut tree, which is now for all practical purposes extinct, pierced his toes. He continued to amass an impressive collection of animals. There was usually at least one dog as a family pet. Mother Mabel tolerated "crawdads" and snakes in the icebox, while a horned toad climbed on her expensive lace curtain to feed on flies. There is a Hines family tale of a time when Mabel went outdoors to do some mending. One of her son's crows nabbed her thimble and flew off with the shiny bauble. George Hines was not much of a hunter, but he did enjoy accompanying his family on local fishing trips. Bob rarely spoke about memories of his mother. Alluding to her strength of character, he recalled that Mabel would bait her own hooks when fishing.

During the summer of 1925, as Bob entered his teenage years, Mabel Hines developed an unshakable fatigue that persisted as the months passed. By December, she began to experience chest discomfort and breathlessness that worsened until she became bedridden. Her symptoms reached a crescendo when Mabel, a Christian Scientist, ordered her older son, Bill, to get to a phone and call the doctor. In this preantibiotic era, there was little medically that could be done to help her. Early Christmas Eve morning, at forty years of age, Mabel died of chronic pericarditis, an inflammation of the membrane that encases the heart, a complication of rheumatic fever. The local newspaper reported "she leaves behind her grief stricken husband and two manly sons." The article continues, "The passing of so young a woman, and especially a mother would at any time be sad, but coming just at the holiday season when every heart should be joyous there is an added note of sorrow in her death."

That Christmas was a solemn holiday for the Hines family. Funeral arrangements included transport of Mabel's body by train to Columbus for her burial in Greenlawn Cemetery on December 26. The memory of Bill's helplessness compounded by his mother's desperation during her final hours haunted him throughout his life. Subliminally Bob's quest in life would be to regain the unconditional love he had received from Mabel. Mindful of the constant presence of Mabel's death in the family home, George Hines moved his sons from their house on Napoleon Street to a new home on West State Street. George never remarried after the death of his beloved wife, believing that he could not surpass the love he felt for Mabel. Juggling a work week of six days, George Hines assumed the role of single parent for his two teenage sons. The three men formed a family nucleus devoid of a maternal influence. One summer when finances were tight, there was a surplus of cabbage in the garden. The vegetable appeared on the menu for all three meals of the day throughout the week. Thus, Bob eschewed cabbage throughout his adulthood.

Bob sublimated his grief over the loss of his cherished mother by way of two constructive channels: with his menagerie of animals and by becoming a Boy Scout. George Hines continued to encourage his son's expanding collection of pets insofar as the animals remained well fed and their cages kept clean. The assortment of animals included fish, snakes, turtles, quail, crows, owls, woodchucks, skunks, opossums, raccoons, foxes, and several species of ducks. "Most of these... were captives.... I could handle them, but I won't say they were pets. They weren't all tame," Hines later reminisced. "In fact, some I just barely had under control." His close association with these animal counterparts acquainted the young man with their idiosyncratic habits and quirks. Bob learned to recognize the individuality of animals, which enhanced his artwork later in life. Once while trapping in the Fremont area, Hines was disturbed to learn that he had caught a mother skunk while her babies remained in the vicinity. Bob talked to the skunk and disarmed her so that he could step on the trap and free her. He considered the event a personal triumph because the animal never sprayed him in defense of her young.

In his youth, Bob also found companionship in the Boy Scouts. He was familiar with the Scouts as his brother had previously joined the local troop. Because there were no Cub Scouts in the Fremont area, Bob was eager to turn twelve so he could enter the fraternity of the Scouts. Like many boys of his generation, he acquired an inspiration for nature through the writings of Ernest Thompson Seton. Bob related to Seton's tales of Indian boys with their lore of the outdoors and their respect for all forms of life. Once while at Scout camp, another boy bullied Bob into giving him a potato. As though reenacting something from the pages of a Seton story, Bob acquiesced, but he slyly gave his adversary the root of a jack-in-the-pulpit, which bears a harsh, caustic component in its tissues.

When Hines joined the Hayes Council, the rule was that a Scout could not begin to work on merit badges until he was a first-class Scout. Bernard Armstrong, the local Scout leader, invited Bob, then a second-class Scout, on a bird walk. The bird study merit badge was a requirement for becoming an Eagle Scout. To qualify for this particular merit badge, a Scout needed to identify forty birds in the field. Once a boy identified an individual species, no one else that day could claim that bird as his identification. Bob remembered, "I got my 40 birds in one morning, and then [Armstrong] told me not to come anymore, because I spoiled everybody else's chances."

Hines relished the acceptance that he received in the Boy Scouts. His first scouting award occurred during a two-week stint at the newly opened Camp Miakonda near the Ohio–Michigan state line. Miakonda, still active in 2011, was the oldest Boy Scout camp in Ohio. The name came from the Native American word for "crescent moon." The emblem bears a slender crescent for the "C" in Camp. At Miakonda, Bob found a yellow-fringed orchis, a first-time record for the wild orchid in northwestern Ohio. He also located an ovenbird's nest within ten feet of the Council Ring. Bob had the camp director alter the walk to the Council Ring so that the traffic would not disturb the nest. Beginning in 1924, camp leaders presented the Peter Navarre award to an outstanding Scout. A local historical figure in the Toledo, Ohio, area, Navarre was a fur trader who became a military scout, delivering messages for the Americans during the War of 1812. At the end of the first week of camp, Director Pierce announced from the Council Ring that for the first time in the history of the camp two PN awards were in order that night. Bob was sitting in the back row with three other Scouts from Fremont. When he heard about the second award, he stood and began to walk toward the Council Ring. One of Bob's fellow Fremont Scouts grabbed his shirt and asked him where he was going. With no knowledge of the recipient, Hines replied, "I'm going down to get one of those." As Bob entered the Council Ring, he heard his name announced. The patch is a circular design of two shades of gray flannel stitched together such that the letters "PN" nestle in the concavity of the camp's crescent. Receiving the distinction of outstanding Scout was a tonic for Bob's tender young ego.

While still a teenager, Bob became a nature instructor at three Boy Scout camps including a free summer camp on Kelleys Island in Lake Erie. He was one of the first Scouts in his state to earn the newly available journalism merit badge. Considering a career in journalism, young Bob became a cub reporter for the local newspaper, the *Fremont Daily News*. He wrote a weekly column that frequently featured some aspect of natural history. One such feature details a hike to nearby Brady's Island, a lenticular-shaped tract afloat in the Sandusky River, accessible by two railroad trestles. In an effort to describe the historical significance of the island's name, the first paragraph begins in an awkward manner with a plethora of comma splices. However, the piece reveals a youthful zeal for the small, the commonplace, and the ordinary.

In December 1926, Bob stopped at the *Daily News* office to deliver his article, but he neglected to mention his involvement in a heroic rescue effort. Hence, the *Fremont News Messenger*, the competing newspaper in town, preempted details of the event. A local teamster dismounted a team of two horses in downtown Fremont without securing the animals. The startled horses began running several blocks through the city streets. Bob had just left his school as the frantic animals passed him headed toward a group of school children. Fourteen years old, Hines made a flying leap onto the wagon frame attempting to reach the reins, hanging upside down between the agitated horses. As the boy began to gain control over the team, they turned onto a side street before colliding with a truck transporting several crates of live turkeys. The truck overturned, but its driver was not injured. Bob was thrown off the wagon frame, but he, too, was uninjured. The driver of a bakery wagon finally stopped the team of horses, both of which were hurt in the bedlam. The newspaper report of the incident concludes: "The truck load of turkeys was scattered about the street[,] and there was a merry chase for several minutes to recapture the birds which, seemingly realizing that they were headed for the Christmas dinner table, started to make a getaway."

Bob made a meteoric rise in the Boy Scouts, attaining the Eagle Scout level three years to the day of joining the Hayes Council. Bob's brother William, also an Eagle Scout, secured the eagle pin onto Bob's uniform during the ceremony held at City Hall. Their father, George Hines, gave some remarks to the younger boys. Bob eventually earned the Eagle Scout with Silver Palm, designating fifteen additional merit badges above the twenty-one required for the Eagle Scout. As scoutmaster George Hines insisted, both of his sons took their merit badge examinations twice to avoid any suspicion of favoritism in the troop.

The Fremont troop was an active organization with three sets of brothers, all Eagle Scouts. The boys participated in tournaments and field meets. Bob recalled, "because I was so little and weighed so little, they would throw me first over the wall for wall scaling, and then I would be on top of the pyramid to do the signaling." In three years, the Fremont troop lost just one contest. Activities included wig wag signaling and flag semaphore. The troop went on camping trips practically every month, walking up and down the Sandusky River. Once they swam across the river in March. Three years before his death, Bob recalled, "I could have posed for Gainesborough's Blue Boy. I was cold! We, in the rain, found an old log, cut it open and got dry wood... and we made fire by friction. I had a shoelace and a knife, and that's all it takes.... I think I could still do it. Maybe I'm too weak to run the bow, but I know how."

Bob had one major disappointment as a Scout. He learned that adventurer and filmmaker Martin Johnson planned to cooperate with the Boy Scouts by taking two Scouts on an African safari. The prerequisites were that the candidates had to be high ranking and that they could draw and write well. Hines always liked to draw, was writing a weekly column for the local newspaper, and was one of the highest-ranking Scouts for a time in the state. George Hines agreed to his son's interest to travel abroad. The local Scout executive nominated Bob to represent Ohio, but his application was rejected because he was about six months over the age limit. Johnson later took three boys, not two, to Africa; one of them, the son of a national Scout commissioner, was older than Hines.

In future years, Hines paid his indebtedness to the Boy Scouts by illustrating three merit badge handbooks—*Nature*, *Fishing*, and *Wildlife Management*.

Bob continued to pursue his outdoor interests during his formative years in the Fremont area. Hines recalled, "The first wild duck I ever shot was a black duck at Sandusky Bay." He continues, "I learned to hunt ducks educated by an old market hunter in the Sandusky Bay, and he used to blow the heck out of me if I did it wrong. And he said you're not supposed to go barrel stretching or sky shooting, you wait until you can see the eye of the duck.

If you're looking for it, you can see it at forty yards, and that bird's within range... because most shotguns are not any good beyond that."

Hines attended Fremont High School. Although a loner at heart, he displayed a pleasant, personable demeanor that facilitated his involvement in several extracurricular clubs including Hi-Y, science, and Spanish (he was president of the latter during his senior year). He was the class treasurer during his junior year. Also a member of the Dramatic Club, he appeared in two class plays during his senior year. This experience may have contributed to his ease in public speaking, which he enjoyed later in his public career. Bob was an assistant art editor for the senior class yearbook. In what is possibly his first published illustration, the *1928 Croghan* yearbook features one of his drawings, a medieval hunting scene. The image depicts two men on horseback, their pack of hounds pursuing a hare. Also in the yearbook is a photo of Mary Williams, the school's art teacher. She has an oval face with soft features topped with brunette finger waves; her expression is direct and no nonsense. Miss Williams would later facilitate Bob's entry into an art career.

George Hines recalled: "One of [Bob's] teachers came to me and told me early that I should not waste my son's life by having him do anything but paint." Bob was a good, solid student with a tendency for his grades to slip ever so slightly as the year progressed. His report cards show surprisingly few absences, suggesting a level of self-discipline that may have been honed by his years as a Boy Scout.

The Class Prophecy section of the yearbook predicts, "Bob Hines has created a big sensation by discovering a new kind of butterfly. It's a cross between a bird and a bumble bee. He is head of the biology department at Vassar. Bob always did like girls."

Brother William recently completed a year of college at Ohio State University but had to withdraw because of financial reasons. Bob very well could have gone on for a higher education, but he understood that his father could not afford to have one son, let alone two, in college.

Accompanying Bob's senior photo is the verse "The mind of a sage, and the soul of a boy." At sixteen years of age, he was fresh faced, jug eared, less than one hundred pounds in weight, and ready to find his niche in life.

Chapter 2

Artwork to Educate

With few prospects for furthering his formal education, Hines taught himself taxidermy, possibly through a correspondence course. The discipline was a good match for his outdoor interests and creative instincts. Unbeknownst to him, this knowledge would provide valuable insight into the anatomy and motion of his future animal subjects when he became a wildlife artist. He recalled, "I have confidence now in trying to reconstruct making a bird or animal or anything move in any direction I want because they all have the same muscles and bones, they're just different proportions. Weasel and lions have the same muscles, they just move differently." In another interview, Hines added: "A duck might take on any position his bones and muscles will allow. If you know how his wings work, you'll know what he can do and what he can't do." As with any new task, there was a learning curve as he refined his skill. "The first animals I mounted wouldn't have been recognized by their own mothers," he reminisced. After Hines eviscerated the creature, he found himself sketching the carcass to reinforce its anatomy. "That way I knew where the bones were and how the muscles moved."

By the autumn of 1933, Bob remained active as an assistant Scout master with the local troop 307. After an outing with the Scouts, he "spent the evening skinning a female wood duck, one of the rarest and most beautiful birds in this section. It was the first of the species I have ever prepared." Two days later he added, “The female wood duck is mounted, quite to my satisfaction, too. Blood clots on either flank, both cheeks, and the neck required washing, but every feather is clean and in place. . . . It stands as the best bird I have ever put up. To me it seems odd that such a rare bird should be as easy to mount as any other. For no particular reason, I expected unusual specimens to be difficult to mount.”

Two local men hunting ducks on nearby Sandusky Bay were “arrested by the sight of a living thunderbolt dropping out of the clouds onto their live decoys. ‘A hawk,’ they cried, and one fired, so that the feathered destroyer was pierced and broken in a dozen places, and fell dead where he would have killed. The mighty claws of the bird were too huge, the great wings too regal; this was no ordinary hawk, but an eagle, inconspicuous in immature plumage, but an eagle still.” The duo brought the bird to Hines’s taxidermy shop where he marveled at “the truly enormous spread of wing, measured twice, and the greatest I have ever tabulated, was 7 feet, 9 inches.” Bob added this postscript: “The eagle proved female. Her appetite for duck is explained by an empty stomach.”

Hines admitted, “I am confident of my work on birds; small animals sometimes present difficulties.” By Thanksgiving 1933, he documented, “Since the first day of hunting season I have mounted eight pheasants, five Hungarian partridges, a drake pintail, a ruffed grouse, a sparrow hawk, and today a telephone call promised a short-eared owl.” One week later, Bob wrote, “Tonight a young male fox squirrel, the victim of a machine, was handed in. The winter pelt is thick & long.” Around this same time a colleague sent Bob an adult female red-tailed hawk. Hines documented, “The poor bird was still alive, though only feebly, since it was suffering from a fractured skull. Such a wild beauty! I killed it with my hands as I walked along, and was glad when at last it went limp. Such futile struggles as it made! I wish it were alive and free. . . . A hawk’s heritage is an open sky and lack of human pursuit . . . mute testimony of its qualities was offered by the opened stomach—it contained a solid pellet of field mouse and bones.”

Households had less discretionary spending as the Great Depression settled in with widespread unemployment. A hunter might bring in his prized trophy specimen to the shop with grand plans to preserve the creature for posterity. However, the next time Hines saw him this individual might cross the street to avoid talking to Hines because the fellow would not have enough money to pay him for his services. Bob recalled during the Depression he once "got the enormous price of $10 for mounting a pheasant." George Hines urged Bob to promote his taxidermy skills. Bob displayed his handiwork in the windows of the local Hill's Shoe Repair shop and the Fremont Hardware Company. He confided to his journal, "Taxidermy and its attendant demands, odors and dirt, [Father] dislikes, nor do I blame his point of view. Material success is his one aim for me; I see wealth and beauty in the sheen of a hawk's wing, success in a well mounted animal, reward in the fervent praise of a sportsman; yet he is right—these are not what bread and butter are bought with." Hines practiced the trade for about a decade until two other taxidermists in town began to reduce their prices. He decided to close his shop and gave a number of mounted specimens to the Boy Scouts.

As the economy continued to darken, Hines accepted whatever manual labor might provide some intermittent income. Uneducated and untrained, Bob recorded his despair: "Odd jobs are hardly to be considered, they are so few. Regular work I have been unable to find—that is something partly to be blamed on ill luck, and partly, I admit, on my lack of perseverance. I do not have the stuff I ought to; I lack nearly everything that dreams are founded on." One summer he took care of seventeen lawns. The local custom was to roll yards in the spring to level the turf. This was quite a chore for Bob, who weighed ninety-eight pounds when he graduated from high school. The roller was far heavier than its young operator. He also used a manual reel-type mower, earning twenty-five cents per yard for his efforts. For six years, Bob took on an assortment of odd jobs. Years later, on his application for federal employment, he includes a laundry list of these seemingly endless mundane duties concluding the summary with five etc.'s, each separated by ellipses.

With his days as a high school cub reporter behind him, Bob began keeping a written journal late in 1933. He admitted, "The writing, too, has slipped. My thoughts, once well trained and orderly, seem now to lack coherence. One of the real reasons I am keeping these pages is to regain the command I should have, as well as to promote orderliness and regularity." One exercise describes a thimble as "a diminutive argentous truncated cone inverted on its summit and semi-perforated with symmetrical indentations." Hines's journal entries reflect a restlessness common to many members of his generation during the uncertainty of this decade of the Great Depression. Bob had inquired about the Civilian Conservation Corps (CCC), the brainchild of newly elected President Franklin D. Roosevelt. The CCC offered unemployed young men room and board as well as a nominal income for their labor in federally funded projects. A local recruitment effort through the Findlay, Ohio, office offered the promise of an assignment with a reforestation project at Kentucky's Camp Knox, an ideal match for Bob's outdoor interests. As Hines completed an application for the Corps, he confidently documented his involvement with the Boy Scouts, detailing his Eagle Scout status with Silver Palm as well as his assistant Scout master duties. Bob opined to his journal, "Whatever preparation is necessary will be worthwhile, for the C.C.C. is a chance for larger things."

After "a long, jostling truck ride to Findlay with other candidates," the young men were ordered to strip bare in the armory where the air "was so smoke filled that objects at the opposite end were veiled as in a fog." Bob recalled, "salty perspiration ran down my upper arms and dripped from my elbows. . . ." A civilian doctor evaluating the men for skin and posture defects recorded "psoriasis" on Hines's medical form. A uniformed medical officer barked, "Alright Hines, put your clothes on, you're rejected." His self-confidence shattered, Bob thought, "I wonder if I can ever get that phrase out of my mind." Despite his outward disregard of the rejection in the company of the other candidates, privately Bob confessed, "My ill luck seemed a near catastrophe."

Along with many of his peers from the northwestern corner of Ohio, Hines was drawn to the vortex of the Rainbow Gardens, a popular nightspot in Fremont. White-jacketed waiters attended to the patrons who danced on marble floors in the cavernous space to the swing music of traveling bands. The majority of Bob's journal entries record his visits to the Gardens with a succession of young women. "Everybody does something that they take pride in. I like to dance," he declared. His records of the evenings spent at the Gardens are largely factual. Perhaps his most suggestive entry is: "Jenny came out to me, and we drove away together. . . . What we did concerns us alone. I felt then, and I feel the same way now, that I could hold her in my arms much longer than I did." Bob predicted that the Rainbow Gardens would become even busier with the repeal of Prohibition in December 1933.

Late in 1934, Hines obtained his first regular employment at Ray Lemon's Little Restaurant, housed in the busy Fremont Greyhound Bus station. Bob recalled, "I would bake 25 pies on a Saturday night. I regularly roasted anywhere from two to four hams, big whole hind end of a hog, and sometimes two steamship rounds of beef." The work was twelve hours a day, seven days a week, for a weekly pay of $19. Another benefit was that he gained seven pounds while working there. During one restive moment, Hines went outside of the bus station to pelt eggs at its brick chimney. L. D. McGrady, the cook, rebuked Bob, reminding him that the owner of the establishment would find no humor in wasting food, especially with the Great Depression in progress.

After sixteen months, Hines left the restaurant to work at Herbrand Corporation, the local drop forge plant that manufactured tools, automobile parts, and accessories. There may have been some nepotism at play as Bob's father was a foreman at Herbrand, which was a major employer in the Fremont area. Bob inspected shipping orders, completed invoices, and supervised the nightly loading of about 110 tons of merchandise on trucks for transport. He usually packed a tablet in his lunch box for sketching during break time. The stress of a work schedule with little flexibility, being awake all night when the body craves rest, and rigid shipping deadlines that left little room for error conspired against Bob's physical health to the point that he developed "mucus colitis." Hines repeated his doctor's advice: "Well, look, you can keep on there and live a short life, or you can get out of there and do something else and live a while."

In an attempt to adopt a less stressful lifestyle, Bob decided to turn to drawing, a hobby he always enjoyed. The act of composing artwork fulfilled his creative instincts, but it also brought him a measure of comfort. Drawing kindled fond memories of those early boyhood days when his childlike images pleased his dear mother as she grieved over the death of her infant daughter. By early 1934, Bob registered for an art course with the Federal Schools of Minneapolis, which had a representative in Toledo, Ohio. Hines's entry for Thursday, February 1 states: "The first instructions on the drawing lessons arrived today along with equipment and supplies. I am well satisfied." Bob submitted a set of dog drawings that the *Columbus Sunday Dispatch* printed in one of its color comic sections in 1936. His application for federal employment states that he left employment at Herbrand in September 1937; the reason for leaving is "to study art." An undated newspaper clipping from Hines's papers states that he saved enough money to tide him over financially until he could refine his art skills.

In a publicized case from 1938, a hunter in nearby Tiffin, Ohio, shot a melanistic or dark phase pheasant. Not knowing what it was, the man left the dead bird in the field. This act galvanized Bob to consider drawing wildlife so that he could educate the public. As Hines's concept of a career change began to coalesce, he noted in 1939 that Ohio's newly elected governor, John Bricker, appointed Don Waters as the state conservation commissioner. Despite his duties in Columbus, Waters maintained his home in Elmore, about fourteen miles from Fremont. Hines contacted Waters and arranged a meeting at his Elmore residence on a Saturday to explore opportunities in wildlife art. Bob arrived with a stack of drawings under his arm. To Hines's delight, he learned that Waters had attempted to draw wildlife himself but could not do so to his own satisfaction. Well over six feet in height, Waters had a broad physique and a dignified manner. A photograph of him shows a high frontal hairline, a cleft chin, and round spectacles that give him an owlish appearance. Waters spread the drawings on the floor and then got on his hands and knees to examine them closely.

After an interval of intense concentration, he looked up at Hines and asked him, "Can you come to work next Friday?"

Why Waters chose Friday as a starting day was a riddle that perpetually tickled Hines: "It wasn't the end of a pay period or anything." The salary would be $2,200 a year.

Upon accepting the new job, Hines learned that his first assignment would be to paint in oils the background for a planned set of natural habitat groups. Waters asked, "Can you handle it?"

Hines replied affirmatively, even though he later revealed, "I had never done an oil painting in my life, but I was cocky enough to say yes, I could, and I knew that I could do the taxidermy because I had been doing that for ten years."

Bob turned to Mary Williams, his former art teacher at Fremont High School. Although he had graduated eleven years prior, Williams allowed him to return to her classroom. From Monday to Thursday, while she circulated throughout the room to teach her current students, she would give tips to Hines about the basics of oil painting as well as composing a painting. He never took a formal art course after high school. In this four-day refresher course, Hines learned enough about oil painting to serve him the remainder of his professional art career. On that Friday in February 1939, Bob began his employment with the Ohio Division of Conservation and Natural Resources in Columbus.

The first project, a set of detailed dioramas, was a success. Hines created five glass-fronted vignettes depicting wildlife found in Ohio: a grouping of five Hungarian (or gray) partridges feeding in a snowy field, the background with a trompe l'oeil wire fence leading the eye back to the gable of a barn in the distance; a drake mallard with a male red-winged blackbird displaying its epaulets among the cat tails at the edge of a marsh, a painted rendition of a muskrat aside its reedy mound in the background; a pair of ring-necked pheasants in a grassy field; a trio of gray squirrels scampering in a deciduous forest; and an underwater view of various game fish in a vertical cross section of an Ohio pond. During the Depression, these dioramas were valued at $900 apiece. Conservation officers would haul them on trucks throughout the state for the public to view at various events. Hines said, "We had an underwater pond scene, and to make it look proper, I had an airbrush and faintly filmed the inside of the glass on the front. The lights burned out on the inside, and over in Dayton, one of the game wardens said, 'Oh, this glass is dirty,' and he took all the paint off the inside, and it looked like clear glass, and it destroyed the whole effect." By 1950, the *Ohio Conservation Bulletin* noted, "These dioramas have been displayed at county fairs, sportsmen's shows, and special events all over the state, but throngs of spectators continue to visit them time after time."

Hines had a more personal matter to pursue. While swimming in Lake Erie, he became infatuated with a lifeguard named Edna. Feigning that he could not swim, the young woman gave him some private swimming instruction. Their friendship soon blossomed into a romance.

Edna Delores Beatty was born in Fremont in November 1911, the only child of Howard Beatty, a retired lumber merchant, and his wife, the former Vera Posey. Rheumatic fever was a complication that marked Edna's early childhood. In this preantibiotic era, frequent trips to Florida for recuperation in the sun and warmer climate interrupted her education. Although she was chronologically older than Bob, Edna did not graduate from Fremont High School until 1930. She enrolled at Florida State College for Women in Tallahassee, majoring in physical education. Despite her previous health issues, Edna led a very active athletic lifestyle in college, participating in baseball, track, tennis, swimming, and basketball. During her senior year, she was president of the college athletic club.

In her graduating class of 1934, Edna was the only student from Ohio, and one of two students outside the deep southern states. Her senior portrait shows her brunette hair in a short cut common to many of her fellow classmates. Attractive, but perhaps not a classic beauty, her salient facial features suggest a similar inner strength. The fact that Edna's parents could afford her college education implies that the Beatty's were better off financially than the George Hines family. After graduation, Edna accepted a job offer to teach physical education in Adrian, Michigan. Bob and Edna both had their hometown of Fremont as a common denominator. However, the history of Edna's rheumatic fever and her prominent looks must have subconsciously reminded Bob of his late mother. As an only child, Edna was the focal point of her parents' lives. Vera Beatty's controlling parenting style verged on suffocation. It would be an understatement to say that Howard and Vera Beatty were shocked to learn that their daughter, athletic and college educated during the Great Depression, traveled to Cincinnati then crossed into Kentucky to elope with a young artist. There was a precipitous chill toward their new son-in-law that never abated.

For several months after their marriage, the newlyweds lived apart with Edna's teaching in Adrian, Michigan, and Bob's working in Columbus. During this time of separation, Hines became involved in a prank that caused him embarrassment and could have threatened his employment considering the social conformity of the time. According to his description of the incident, there was a woman by the name of Martha who worked in the restaurant below his apartment. Martha reportedly dared Hines to dress in her clothes and then join her at a drama club event at Ohio State University. On a Saturday night in early March 1940, he did so expecting to meet Martha there, but she never made an appearance. Hines went to the back of the balcony, where he sat rows away from the nearest audience members. Employees at the theater notified a detective who was in the building; this man approached the end of the row where Hines sat. Feeling uncomfortable, Bob left the building while the detective followed him outside. He detained Hines, calling "a uniformed cop," who in turn took Bob to the police station for questioning. Hines posted a $25 fine but was assured it was not a formal arrest. The following Monday morning Edna accompanied Bob to the police court where any charges were dropped. To his chagrin, Hines not only had to divulge the details of imbroglio to his superiors at the Ohio Division of Conservation, but he later included a written statement directed to the US Civil Service Commission that became a permanent part of his personnel file after he joined the federal government.

Aside from innate talent, Hines's observant nature included a keen attention to detail of pose or plumage as well as a sharp recollection of outdoor lore. Tom Duncan vividly remembered the time he and Hines had exited the north side of the Interior Building in Washington, DC, and had entered a small park. As they were walking, a small sparrow flew by. Bob identified the passing bird on the wing, pointing out its field marks. Duncan asked, "How did you see that? That bird was flying 30 miles an hour!" To which Hines replied, "this was just one of those things that [I] learned to do when [I] was younger."

Hines's powers of observation did not diminish even as he approached retirement age. In 1979, Charles Cadieux invited Bob and Pete Anastasi to his home in Albuquerque, New Mexico, for a fishing trip to Mexico's Bahia Kino. The plan was for Cadieux to drive a pickup truck while his guests lounged in a camper secured to the bed of the vehicle. There was an intercom phone for the driver to communicate with the camper. Bob and Pete were relaxing in the camper, mesmerized as the pavement tapered off into a slender ribbon behind them. Pete recalls that Hines bolted upright and yelled, "Aplomado falcon! Stop the truck!" Bob snatched the intercom; dismayed to find it dead, he began to pound on the front wall of the camper. By the time Cadieux recognized the commotion and pulled over alongside the road, the bird was long gone. Hines had recognized the falcon perched on the telephone line as they were traveling at full highway speed. It was a parting glance, but, nonetheless, he could finally say that he had seen all of the North American species of falcons.

Hines began a new animal drawing with some abstract pencil strokes. "I begin with a feeling, an idea. Then I draw a few lines and circles to create an impression. You can create power just by drawing lines." Within time, he might have a few pages of sketches. "These are my shorthand notes. They won't mean much to someone else, but this is what I work from. Then I'll choose one of these according to the impression I'm trying to convey." Two features assumed priority. The eye reveals the personality of the animal. "If the eye isn't alive, then you've failed as an artist," Hines shared with a journalist. Secondly, the backbone, which supports the extremities, determines the pose and drama of the piece. "The spine governs the whole body movement. . . . I try to do an animal the way it looks to me. My first concern is accuracy, conveying an honest impression of an animal and its habitat. But I believe you can show fact and make it attractive. By suggested movement, you can give an animal power or weakness. Depending on the stance, you can make him dance or sing."

As the state wildlife artist, Hines composed—writing and illustrating—"Under Ohio Skies," a weekly feature that debuted in 1942 and appeared in nearly three hundred Ohio newspapers. His boss might suggest facts to include, which Hines would condense into concise bullet points. He would then meticulously ink the entire piece with a fine crow quill pen. The division distributed mats containing an entire month's material to the participating newspapers. Each column educated its readers about some aspect of outdoor lore with the current state laws or natural history factoids. "Buckeye Bill," an anthropomorphized, bipedal raccoon, was the mascot narrator of the series. Hines had a penchant for the raccoon, and he chose to paint the animal on his office signboard after he joined the federal government. Bob admired the agility and adaptability of the raccoon. Its bandit mask became a symbol of Hines's attempts to disguise his own private pain, including his inadequacies as an artist, a spouse, and later a parent.

"Under Ohio Skies" is a time capsule of its era. The modern reader might be disquieted to read about predator control and bounties for "foxes and other vermin." During the World War II years, there are several references to war bonds and victory gardens. Outdoor enthusiasts know to extinguish a lit match by breaking it in half, thereby snuffing the burning head to avoid accidental fires. Hines reinforces this by depicting a smoking match broken into a shape that corresponds to the "V" in victory. In another column, the open season on the harvest of snapping turtles provided an alternative to the rationing of fresh meats. A third feature reminds its readers of the contributions that individual citizens could make to the war effort—waterfowl hunters could send feathers to insulate vests and sleeping bags for the servicemen; hunters could report scrap metal that they found in out-of-the-way places for recycling; and fats from prepared wild game could be saved for use in the manufacture of ammunition. "Under Ohio Skies" also served as a vehicle for the seeds of environmental stewardship, which entered the national lexicon a generation later.

The *Ohio Conservation Bulletin* was the monthly periodical from the Ohio Conservation Division. Oliver Hartley was its editor as well as the head of public relations during Hines's tenure in the division. During the 1940s, there were some fifty thousand subscribers. The cost of the *Bulletin* was ten cents per copy or one dollar for a year's subscription. (In 1945, there was a special offer of fifty cents per year, two years for one dollar, or three years for $1.20.) A 1941 issue refers to the cover art of an airborne covey of quail "by our young Bob Hines. In our long experience in the publishing business, and dabbling some in art, we have never seen such wonderful improvement and rich endowment of talent as this lad has displayed in so short a time. Bob attended no art school, he's just naturally gifted. He's a comer." Despite its modest black-and-white photographs, the *Bulletin* features a nicely balanced layout. Ed Dodds, creator of the comic strip "Mark Trail," wrote a letter to the editor "to congratulate you on [the *Bulletin*'s] setup and the splendid work being done by Bob Hines."

As staff artist, Hines would often illustrate the title heading of an article, perhaps hand lettering the script. Frequently, his artwork would be featured on the front cover with a subtle touch of humor to Hines's compositions. One July issue has three inquisitive raccoons examining a small red rocket with a burning fuse. One can imagine what their reaction will be in a few seconds when the fuse ignites the missile. The editor refers to the image as a "fantastic pictorial representation, which radiates Independence Day spirit in lighter vein." Another cover shows two hounds in the background pursuing a raccoon about to leap onto a tree trunk; in the foreground, out of sight of the dogs, is a wary skunk with its bushy tail raised in preparation for the approaching encounter.

An uncredited photograph of Hines appears on two covers. His lean body and handsome looks give the impression of an Everyman for outdoors Ohio. Occasionally Bob would author an article himself for inclusion in the *Bulletin*. In one such piece on Ohio snakes, he notes, "There is a sort of natural instinct of repugnance toward snakes of any kind by most people, but this attitude should not be permitted to build up into ungrounded fear, and the tendency to see nothing of the beauties of nature by reason of keeping a close focused watchout for reptiles." In another article, Hines writes about hunting Hungarian partridges with two partners, his director and a former Army sharpshooter, along with Hines's retriever, Sally. As the story begins, "[I]t was the last day of the bird season last fall. Now any bird shooter can tell you that you shouldn't expect too much on the last day, because the birds have been flushed from here to breakfast and shot from all angles, and any score is just plain gravy." Bob describes the partridges as "the fastest flying cornfield targets you will ever come up against." Hines bagged "a cock bird, an old one judging from the rounded wingtips, fat and heavy from rich food," loading the bird with his full shotgun blast. Bryan, the Army veteran, downed another bird with a single bead to its neck. He chastised Bob, "Sure you centered your bird and you'll eat buckshot. I lead mine and you'll not find him all loaded with shot because of it. . . . You know, I'm a little disappointed. I was really shooting for his head and here I hit him in the neck."

The inside panel of the front cover usually has a monochromatic Hines piece that highlights a particular subject of interest to the sportsman. Bob would ink the illustration in a similar style to "Under Ohio Skies," but with a bit more detail. One issue from 1947 titled "They Swim, They Walk, but the Air is Their True Element" features the latest research of ducks in flight using state-of-the-art fast action photography. With step-by-step illustrations, Hines details "Mallards don't jump, they fly out of the water. An alarmed drake unfolds his wings, lays them flat on the water, thrusts vigorously, starts the upbeat, and is airborne all within one half second of time." Working for the Conservation Division gave Hines exposure to new findings. He would store these details about the flying mallard and incorporate them again in the next decade when he painted a large mural depicting a flock of mallard ducks arising from a snowy winter pond.

As Hines perfected his artistic skills, he became proficient in other media—pen and ink, brush and ink, dry brush, scratch board, washes, transparent and tempora watercolors, oils, charcoal, chalk, and pencil. It would only be a matter of time until his talent would extend beyond the boundaries of his home state of Ohio.

Chapter 3

The Pantheon of Waterfowl Artists

Hines was fortunate that his superiors at the Ohio Conservation Division did not discourage personal freelance activities. Beginning in 1939, Bob started a series of profiles on resident animals at the Columbus Zoo, which the *Columbus Sunday Dispatch* intermittently featured in a color full-page spread as part of its weekly comic section. Hines also wrote a short paragraph about each animal to accompany its portrait. The newspaper credited Robert Hines as "an outstanding young Fremont, Ohio, artist."

In 1942, Edna and Bob moved into a house on Glenn Avenue in the Grandview Heights section of Columbus. That same year, Edna gave birth to their first child, a son, John. The inside front cover panel of the August 1942 *Ohio Conservation Bulletin* features Pymatuning Lake, which straddles the Ohio–Pennsylvania state line. Under Hines's customary printed signature, he also inked in "now Father Hines." For a measure of parental pride, a copy of the piece in his scrapbook has a red arrow pointing to the tiny addition with a handwritten notation, "In Honor of 'Johnny.'" A daughter, Nancy, joined the family in 1944. Bob demanded complete silence for his muse of artistry to cast her spell over him, an untenable request with young, exuberant children in the household. He resorted to renting a room in a local office building where he could relish in his solitude as he translated his visions onto paper or canvas.

Hines also had family members of other species, a continuation of his boyhood practice to surround himself with animals. One newspaperman reported, "Mrs. Bob Hines has learned not to be surprised anymore at what she runs across in her home at 1365 Glenn Avenue. It just isn't normal unless some pet skunks, crows, or squirrels are darting about the rooms, or some fish are swimming around in the bathtub. And, preparing breakfast one morning, Mrs. Hines found the refrigerator full of live crawfish!"

Bob adopted an albino crow while visiting the wildlife station at Ohio State University (OSU) on business. The bird "didn't have one black feather on him, pink eyes, pink bill, pink feet. He was one of a strain from central Ohio." Hines was surprised at its small size, then appalled to learn that the young bird had been fed only once a day. "That's like feeding a newborn baby once a day. . . . I took it home, and this was during the meat rationing days after World War II, but that crow had hamburger and eggs. I'll tell you he did pretty well." After the bird died of pneumonia, Hines donated its body to the OSU museum.

As a contributor to the *Ohio Conservation Bulletin* as well as creator of "Under Ohio Skies," Hines became a candidate for membership in the Outdoor Writers Association of America (OWAA), which he officially joined in 1942. President J. Hammond Brown sent a letter to Hines welcoming him to the organization. Brown added, "I want to congratulate you on your new undertaking, 'Under Ohio Skies.' It is well conceived and beautifully executed. . . . Please keep me advised on anything new you do so I can say a word about it. Merit is the foundation for success, but a little publicity is bound to help."

A severe drought threatened wildlife in the American midwest during the Great Depression. In 1934, the US Congress approved the Migratory Bird Hunting Stamp, commonly known as the Federal Duck Stamp, requiring all waterfowl hunters sixteen years of age and older to purchase a stamp prior to the hunting season. Proceeds from the sale of the stamps go toward the purchase or restoration of waterfowl habitat. Hines recalled: "I remember as a duck hunter around Sandusky Bay in northern Ohio, we always [had] to pay a dollar [for a Duck Stamp] to go hunting. I didn't have any idea at that time what it meant or the fact that I should have kept it. I don't think I saved any of the first twelve stamps."

Selection of the annual Duck Stamp design has changed over the years. Initially the Office for Law Enforcement, under the umbrella of the Fish and Wildlife Service (FWS), invited artists to submit their drawings for consideration. In 1944, J. Hammond Brown, president of the OWAA, reported that Walter Weber was to design that year's Federal Duck Stamp. This news alerted Hines to the possibility of a commission. When Bob queried "Ham" Brown about the Duck Stamp design he replied, "Well, why don't you draw one and send it in?" In 1945, Hines submitted two pencil designs—one of shovelers and one of redhead ducks. To Bob's dismay, Owen Gromme's design of three flying shovelers was the selection for that year's stamp.

Ronnie Gascoyne, the assistant chief of law enforcement, returned the artwork with an encouraging letter suggesting that Hines simplify the redhead design by omitting a second flock of ducks in the background and then resubmitting that modified drawing the following year. Bob accepted the criticism and did as he was instructed. His revised version, in pen and ink with a watercolor wash, depicts an airborne drake redhead with outstretched wings and extended legs about to descend alongside a small grouping of three drakes and one hen all floating on the rippled water's surface. Hines reportedly drew this image from memory based on his observation of redhead ducks on the Sandusky River a decade prior.

At noon one day in March 1946, Hines went to the Columbus post office to check his mail. A letter from the FWS quickened his pulse. Opening the envelope, he found a letter from Albert Day, acting director. To his elation, Bob read the first paragraph: "The drawings submitted by the several artists have been carefully examined and it is my pleasure to state the one furnished by you of the five redheads has been accepted for the design of the 1946–47 Migratory Bird Hunting Stamp."

After he completed reading the entire letter, Bob sat on the steps of the post office in disbelief, oblivious to the rush of people around him. "I was the best God-blessed Duck Stamp artist in the whole country, and I knew it because he said so. If I had worn a vest, I'd have popped all the buttons." Nearly fifty years later, Hines's voice cracked with emotion as he recalled, "I knew at that moment about the best happiness I ever had." Bob never forgot that ecstasy as he learned of his achievement. After he became the coordinator for the Duck Stamp competition, he strived to instill that same sense of bliss into each year's winning artist.

The letter from Albert Day concludes with a postscript: "Please do not make any public announcement of this award until we have issued a press release, copy of which will be promptly forwarded to you." Hines wanted to comply with the secrecy clause, but he was beside himself with euphoria. Bob confided in Don Waters, the conservation commissioner, showing him the letter. Hines later recalled, "He pounded his desk, smacked my back so hard I still remember it, and took me to lunch the next day. After the announcement was made in Washington, he had me attend the commissioner's meeting and read the letter and be congratulated."

Hines's stamp, the thirteenth one in the series, bears a monochromatic maroon brown color. With a release date of July 1, 1946, and a purchase price of one dollar, the redhead stamp was the first Duck Stamp to sell over two million copies. The increased sales were a reflection of the number of servicemen returning home after the end of World War II. In an interesting twist of fate, Rachel Carson, then a writer for the FWS Information Office, wrote the official Service press release about the record-breaking sales of Hines's 1946 stamp. After Bob joined the Service, Carson would be his supervisor as well as a friend, colleague, and collaborator.

The *Ohio Conservation Bulletin* for May of that year features a photo of Hines on its cover. Taken at his Glenn Avenue home in Columbus, the image shows Bob nattily attired in a long-sleeved dress shirt, necktie, and sweater vest. He sits working at his drawing table with a pen in his right hand and a cigarette in his left. Discussing Hines in the "Editorial Bulletin Board," Oliver Hartley writes: "He has won the annual national 'duck stamp' contest, in competition with top-flight wildlife artists of the whole country. . . . Eight years ago Bob came into our office with a bundle of sketches and paintings and timidly indicated that he'd like to try his hand at art work for the Division. He had never been to art school, and his samples showed amateurism, but the divine spark of genius glinted through. . . . We again admit that we're proud of his work, and appreciative of pleasant personal relations throughout the years for our professional association."

Hines recorded the history behind his Duck Stamp in a document he playfully titled, "That Lucky 13th Duck Stamp." With that piece he demonstrates humility: "In the 1930's and '40's there were no great rewards for designing the Federal Duck Stamp—no big publicity and certainly no financial rewards. It was just the honor of doing it." Bob even had to pay a dollar to purchase a Duck Stamp bearing his design for himself. Edward Thomas of Abercrombie & Fitch in New York City approached Hines for permission to distribute hand-pulled stone lithograph prints of his design in black ink on white paper. With the first edition of three hundred signed prints, out of the $15 sale price, Hines received $9. Bob recalled, "No big deal—no overnight millionaires. It was just part of doing the stamp. I remember giving prints to my Father and a few friends, especially Mr. Waters." After the first edition sold out, a second edition later became available, but it may not have met the demand of the first edition.

At thirty-four years of age, Hines achieved his goal of becoming a member of the pantheon of Federal Duck Stamp artists. He gained national exposure through his redhead duck design, all because of a few words of encouragement from the president of the OWAA. Membership in that organization broadened his network of contacts, providing yet more opportunities for him to apply his artistry and to travel.

Chapter 4

Alaska Beckons

In 1944, Conservation Commissioner Don Waters instructed Bob Hines to display some of Hines's artwork at the clubhouse during the Grand American Handicap, the annual trap shoot event held at Vandalia, Ohio. Hines happened to be making signs at the Department of Conservation office in Vandalia where the leaders of the Outdoor Writers Association of America (OWAA) were meeting. Bob recalled, "all of a sudden here's Ham Brown, the president, Charlie Gilliam, Henry Davis, the big boys back in the 1930's, and I didn't know it, but there was Frank Dufresne."

Born and reared in New Hampshire, Dufresne never graduated from high school but continued to educate himself through night classes and self-study. He began working as a newspaper reporter in the Boston area. Upon enlisting in the Army, he served with the American Expeditionary Forces in France during World War I. After Dufresne's military discharge, he drifted into Alaska with inchoate goals of reporting and conservation work. By 1921, the US Marshall's Office in Nome appointed him a fur warden with a Deputy US Marshall's rank.

Dufresne wished to transition from law enforcement to wildlife management. He soon applied for employment in the Bureau of Biological Survey, which was under the US Department of Agriculture. On his application, Dufresne detailed his education: "High school. Two Business colleges. Much and varied reading. Own several volumes on natural history—and know them." His ambition shines through on a subsequent personal statement: "Really believe that I could do creditable work in the position applied for, or in any similar position. Am particularly anxious to go through to the top in conservation of America's wildlife. Am sincere in believing that I could give absolute satisfaction and show the ability to receive and profit by every opportunity for advancement offered. Have no desire to finish my days as a deputy fur warden—regard it simply as opening and as an opportunity to show what I can do."

The application apparently impressed Dr. Nelson as he appointed Dufresne fur warden for the Bureau during the autumn of 1923. Nearly one year later, Dufresne revealed foresight regarding his career. "I would like to know what particular course of study I could take up which would make for advancement in the Bureau. . . . I am not impatient nor in the least dissatisfied. My work is of absorbing interest and is continually presenting me with problems that are fascinating 'nuts' to crack. I am simply taking a long look ahead and it has prompted me to this letter."

Dufresne ascended through the government hierarchy. By 1928, as a warden for the Alaska Game Commission, he traveled widely to the far reaches of the territory "about 16,000 miles covered by dog team, and closer to 20,000 by various small watercraft during the summer seasons." His law enforcement duties brought forth seventy-one violations that exacted "$10,000 in furs, $4,800 in fines and penalties, as well as 205 days in jail."

In 1936, he was a logical successor to lead the Alaska Game Commission in Juneau when the Bureau transferred Executive Officer Hugh Terhune to its Washington, DC, office. Dufresne received ringing endorsements, aided by his avuncular manner and stellar ethics. The *Daily Alaska Empire* included an editorial that states: "The new Executive Officer is not only one of the most capable men that could have been chosen for the position but he is what Alaskans refer to as one of their own."

The animals, landscape, and people whom Dufresne met became grist for his writing avocation. He compiled an impressive dossier of newspaper and magazine articles, many of which promoted the territory. His public appearances further elevated the public perception of the Game Commission. By 1944, Dufresne decided to leave Alaska to accept the position as chief of information for the Fish and Wildlife Service (FWS), which because of the wartime crunch in Washington, DC, was headquartered in Chicago. His appointment included a sound approval from Ira Gabrielson, director of the FWS. Commenting on Dufresne's lack of formal education credentials, which Gabrielson wrote "seems to be becoming increasingly a fetish with the Civil Service people," he continued: "Since he has been with the Service, Mr. Dufresne has applied himself diligently and I know from personal experience, and from personal association, that he knows thoroughly the birds and mammals and knows them about as well as most of the Ph.D.'s that have graduated from our universities and colleges with a major in zoology. In fact, his actual knowledge of the habits of birds and mammals is superior to that of most of them." After commenting on Dufresne's writing skills, his knack for public speaking, his use of "out-of-doors" photography and "motion picture films," Gabrielson concludes: "It is not my understanding that lack of formal education is a bar to a man's promotion in the federal government when he has amply demonstrated his ability to do the job."

When Hines offered to drive the visitors to the trap shoot event, he was surprised to learn that Dufresne was sitting next to him in the front seat. "We get in the car, there was six of us all together, and somebody said something about Frank Dufresne, and I said, 'Boy, I'd sure like to meet him,' and he says, 'Well here I am,' and he hits me on the knee, and the car went down on the berm and up the road again."

Hines asked Dufresne to critique his artwork displayed at the clubhouse. On the spot, Dufresne offered Bob—who had not yet even visited Alaska—the opportunity to illustrate his newly written book on Alaskan wildlife. Hines then went to a trap shoot for the OWAA. Ammunition was scarce because of the wartime emergency. Each participant received twenty-five shells. Hines had never shot trap before and missed the first disk. The man coordinating the match told him to hold his gun at the ready and "then holler pull." Bob was so energized by his newest commission that he hit the next twenty-four disks. "I was far off the ground levitating because I'd just gotten this book from the guy from the Fish and Wildlife Service. Gee, I couldn't lose!" Hines won a war bond and a fifth of whiskey. "It was the first whiskey I'd ever had . . . and I was lucky to get it out of there because these outdoor writers are not going to let much whiskey sit around."

With the Dufresne collaboration, Hines fervently researched the assignment; he could not summon details from his personal memory because many of the species were new to him. One plate depicts a polar bear arising from the sea with its left arm raised about to strike a surprised ribbon seal sunning alone on an ice floe. This was an action Hines had never witnessed in nature. He stripped down to his waist, assumed the pose in front of a mirror, and observed which muscles he used. With his knowledge of anatomy from his taxidermy training, he translated the image into bear muscles for the dramatic image. Hines labored on the painting of a leaping grayling. For two months, he revised the freeze-frame image of the colorful fish, airborne with its oversized trailing dorsal fin as it descended onto an insect floating on the water's surface. Never having seen a grayling, Bob worked from a description of the fish translated from an original French reference. Yet in two days, he completed a three-quarter view of a bull moose looking backward over its massive rear haunches at the viewer, a copse of white birch trees in the background. Hines later explained: "I can't explain it except to say I had the moose clearly in mind and it was just a matter of getting it down." He found some irony when the book was released: the publisher had prominently featured the moose image on the frontispiece of the deluxe edition rather than the grayling watercolor that had challenged Hines for so long.

The 1946 release of *Alaska's Animals and Fishes* includes a few pencil sketches, numerous line drawings in ink, and handsomely executed full-color plates. Hines displays a knack for conveying the action in an image as well as the characteristic pose or habit of his subject. This realism in the illustrations effortlessly complements the almost conversational tone of Dufresne's writing, which begins with Alaskan wildlife from the Pleistocene ice age and segues to the modern day. Commenting on Dufresne's style, Edwin Way Teale wrote: "The matter-of-fact title of this book might lead the reader to expect a dry and conventional presentation of facts about the animals and fishes of Alaska. In a sprightly style, with freshness and enthusiasm, the author writes out of first hand experience . . . without any of the stodginess of the textbook. . . . [I]t is an adventure in reading." A review in the OWAA newsletter states: "We don't know much about Bob Hines who did the illustrations, but we don't need to know anything more than this job to list him as 'tops' as a wildlife artist." The review describes the illustrations as "strikingly unusual and alive."

One reviewer in *Alaska Life* magazine wrote: "Fourteen color plates and innumerable pen and ink sketches illustrate the text of this authentic and fascinating book on Alaska's wildlife, written by the territory's number 1 naturalist and former Fish and Game Commissioner. . . . Making his debut as a book illustrator, Bob Hines does a beautiful job, revealing a genuine originality and unerring color sense in his drawings. The majority of outstanding species of big game and game fishes are portrayed in magnificent color and hundreds of superb black-and-whites give an almost complete representation of every animal and fish discussed in the book. . . . The only criticism we can make of this book is that its release date did not comply with our December deadline. It would have made a wonderful Christmas gift for *Alaska Life* readers to give their families and friends, and even themselves. The book sells for $5. It should sell for $10. Buy it!"

Both Frank Dufresne and Bob Hines personally signed 450 copies of a deluxe edition for the Countryman Press. The accompanying slip case refers to the illustrator as "[o]ne of the most talented of young wildlife artists." Shortly thereafter, A. S. Barnes Company, a division of the Countryman Press, released a smaller version consisting of 10,000 copies for general distribution. (A later 1955 printing from Binfords and Mort reproduces the Hines plates in drab black and white rather than color.)

As Dufresne became a mentor to Hines, another opportunity arose for the younger man. The OWAA was sponsoring an Alaska trek in which Dufresne would be one of the trip leaders. Hines used $100 of his proceeds from A. S. Barnes Company for his registration fee. J. Hammond Brown, executive director of the OWAA, compiled a detailed itinerary with travel suggestions. Guns, salmon rods, and typewriters were to be provided. The participants were to bring along their casting rods and fishing lures, flies, and streamers. The attire was to be informal and weather appropriate. (Brown included: "As for liquid refreshments, I am informed that it is just as good and a bit cheaper in Alaska than down here.")

The *Columbus Dispatch* sponsored Hines as its outdoor writer. He was among the forty-six men and at least two women including seven Ohioans who departed Chicago on August 19, 1947, with stops in Seattle and then onto Ketchikan for two days in that southern Alaska town. The participants then traveled through the Inland Passage with stops at Wrangel and Petersburg en route to Juneau, where they divided into smaller groups for six days of "entertainment" (i.e., fishing derbies). On September 2, the group left Juneau for two days in Whitehorse, Yukon Territory, before returning to Chicago by way of Seattle.

Captain Al Monsen piloted the large, silver, four-motor Pan American Talisman DC-4 from Seattle, landing on Annette Island, about twenty miles from Ketchikan. Arriving in Ketchikan, the participants slept in a United Services Organization dormitory on the waterfront. Hors d'oeuvres consisted of morsels from the US–Alaska Fisheries Products laboratory—kippered king salmon, smoked salmon, pickled kelp, Alaska nuggets (deep-fried flaked fish), halibut cheek balls on crackers, and smoked black codfish. Dessert was fresh blueberry pie. Alaska Governor Ernest Gruening, clad in a green plaid wool sport shirt, and Ketchikan Mayor Bob Ellis made an appearance to welcome the travelers. Governor Gruening spoke about his support for annexation of Alaska as a state, detailing the obstacles that were present.

After dividing into small groups, Bob found himself with V. B. "Viv" Gray, outdoor columnist for the *Cleveland Plain Dealer*; Jack Mahoney of the *Miami Herald*; and Bill Ackerman, member of the editorial staff of the magazine *Outdoors*. The four men boarded a float plane named the "Flying Goose Wigeon," which Mayor Ellis piloted. As the aircraft flew between mountain peaks along the Inland Passage, the plane gained altitude and turned eastward crossing over a snow-capped mountain peak. Hines noticed a white mountain goat ascending the summit; as the plane buzzed by, the goat turned abruptly to escape the din. Hines later reported: "Looking down into the valleys and canyons and their lake studded bottoms is like looking down into a vast submarine garden, with the clouds and the mists drifting across like white moss. You are up where the waterfalls are created, and you can see them plunging great distances like waving white ribbons. Frequently, so many are in sight that they cannot be counted, and all of them are so far back of beyond that they are nameless." The passengers flew over an isolated lake tucked between two mountains, the body of water too small for a plane to land on it. The writers pondered if anyone had ever fished at such a remote location.

About forty-five minutes later, Mayor Ellis lowered the airplane practically to tree top level before some tight spirals gave way to a gentle landing onto the surface of Lake Wilson. One shore of the elongated lake is a verdant spine covered with huge Sitka spruces; elevated rocky cliffs mark the opposite shore. Jeff Anderson, the guide from Ketchikan, donned hip boots and carried each passenger on his back to the shore. After Anderson removed the luggage, Ellis signaled farewell as the plane departed.

An open-ended cabin stood about one hundred feet from the lake's bank. Two double-deck bunks stood at the rear of the cabin. A table with two slab benches, some shelves, and a low sheet iron stove comprised the Spartan kitchen. Anderson began cursing as he entered the cabin—the approaching plane frightened a visiting black bear that had torn a bag of sugar, spreading the crystals as well as flour and salt over the table and dirt floor. There was evidence that the bear had also tried to chew into some cans of food. The men pitched in to clean the mess, then quickly fashioned their sleeping bags on dried spruce boughs, rather than traditional fresh branches, topping the split pole cross beams. Unpacking their fishing gear, they hurried to an accessible point on the rocky shore to fish the brisk lake waters. Bob shouted as he hooked a large trout, but lost it when his fishing leader snapped. He then caught two smaller cut-throat trout. As dusk settled in around 10 p.m., the men returned to the cabin for a meal, not of fresh trout, but heated canned beans, sardine sandwiches, and coffee. They turned into their bunks, exhausted but satisfied.

The visiting bear returned to the camp around 4 a.m. Guide Jeff fired his pistol into the air to redirect the bruin. Hines recorded: "Hearing a bear, which might have been a grizzly but wasn't[,] munching and knawing [sic] within a few feet of your sleeping bag is not conducive to sound sleep."

The bear returned yet again later that morning while Bob and Jeff were catching cutthroat trout. "He stood behind a fallen tree and gave us stare for stare, but since this was the first wild bear that I had ever seen, it is certain that I enjoyed it more than he did. [S]ince I was practicing to become a sourdough [a colloquial expression for a seasoned Alaskan prospector], I kept on looking and fishing until Jeff scared him back into the timber with another shot in the air." Back to fishing, Hines concluded: "Our party finally got into the cutthroats with wet and dry flies, and when the Ellis plane returned for us that evening, to fly us back to Ketchikan, we had caught all we could eat and more, leaving some for the next four writers who were to use the camp that night."

The camp was located in the 16-million-acre Tongass National Forest. Hines recorded his impressions of the area:

> *The perpetual rains of this region not only create gigantic trees, shrubs, and flowers, but even drape them in huge strands of moss, sometimes so long that they sway in the wind like the Spanish moss of our warm southland. To see spruces 120 or 130 feet tall festooned in moss is something, but to see an endless forest of them just cannot be described, you have to see it.*
>
> *These giants are six and eight feet through at the butt, and the gloom of their overlapping branches creates a mossy cathedral. Ferns grow higher than your head, fallen and decayed trunks are hosts to growing plants, including a tiny dogwood, the dwarf cornel, which is also found in Ohio. It is almost inconceivable that this is Alaska. The lushness, the green depths; then between two tall trees you can see a snow covered peak. You know then that this is not some tropic rain forest; this is part of our Northland.*

Colleague Jack Mahoney photographed Hines fly fishing on Lake Wilson. On the back of the framed photo, Mahoney wrote the reminder: "This is where the bear came to our camp." Traveling between Ketchikan and Petersburg, the group observed spawning salmon on Kupreanof Island within the Inland Passage. As the adult salmon migrated from the ocean to their freshwater destination, they underwent a physical transformation. Hines reported, "This is the change made by sickness, disease, and wounds, the weird result of banging into rocks while climbing the streams, of narrow escapes from bears, even from wild fights among themselves. I do not remember seeing one fish that was not all scarred. Some of them are minus fins or tail, some have huge slabs of flesh torn out, some have lost an eye, and a great many of them are so white with a deadly fungus that they look like swimming ghosts." Impressed with the eerie sight as bears, wolves, and eagles carried the dead and dying salmon into the forest, Hines concluded, "I like to catch salmon in the salt water, . . . and it is wonderful to see the fish migrate upstream, but having once seen it, I am not anxious to return and see those spawning pools again."

From Juneau, the Pan American DC-4 airplane flew over the Yukon Highway. The visitors had an opportunity to use that road during the next few days. Hines reported: "Here in this part of the Yukon, the road travels in and out of the mountains and is as beautiful a ride as ever I have taken. It is gravel and equal to or better than many of the country roads in Ohio. It is plenty wide enough for two trucks to pass, and the berms are clear and broad beyond the road bed. One particular item that I noticed and appreciated here was that in night travel, every car we passed always dimmed the lights at our approach, a highway courtesy sometimes lacking back in the states." Hines's party of eighteen stayed overnight at the Marsh Lake Lodge. He wrote: "We arrived at dusk, almost too late for fishing, but five of us diehards dashed out in a futile attempt to catch grayling, the dainty, sweet tasting fish that lives in these headwaters of the Yukon River. All I caught was a two-foot long pike, but landing him on the slim, 3X grayling leader was fun." Dinner that night at the lodge was caribou roast along with sourdough bread "baked on the spot. It is not only decent, it is good, and I really ate plenty of it."

As the trek approached its conclusion, Hines was determined to capture a grayling, which he describes as "the fish found only in the gin-clear Arctic and sub-Arctic waters, this species of grayling has been described as a prince among fishes and one poetical Frenchman pictured him as the fish that feeds on gold. The dorsal[,] or back, fin of the male is huge, huge enough to earn him the name of 'signifer,' meaning standard bearer[,] and he can fold and unfold it, wave it, bend it and flash its brilliant colors like a man waving a flag." Despite the success of other writers in catching a grayling, Hines remained discouraged. He approached Frank Dufresne, whom Bob described as "one of the guiding lights of our trip." Dufresne offered to intervene by arranging a side trip with a pilot, a guide, and two other writers in addition to Hines. Reaching their destination, the party was dismayed to find the stream milky with sediment, no grayling apparent. The party then hopscotched to six other locations until it reached the confluence of Taguish River into Marsh Lake.

Hines still had no success, until the guide suggested fishing from a rustic bridge about twelve feet off the water. It was an unconventional way to catch grayling, but with a little practice, the party was able to hook about 150 grayling in ninety minutes. Hines concluded, "fishing is like living . . . you have to keep trying."

On their return leg with a stop in Juneau, the group met again with Captain Al Monsen who first flew them into Alaska. The writers had an uneventful return to their respective homes back in the lower forty-eight states. Shortly after their arrival came the tragic news that the Pan American Talisman DC-4 that had transported them from Seattle to Ketchikan crashed into a mountainside on its approach to Annette Island, killing Captain Monsen, thirteen passengers, and a crew of five that included two stewardesses who had attended to the writers on their initial flight into Alaska. Strangely a mailbag on the Talisman contained a letter from OWAA president J. Hammond Brown to Earl Ohmer, chairman of the Alaska Game Commission. This letter was one of the few pieces of mail that escaped the fiery crash.

Hines wrote five articles for his benefactor, the *Columbus Dispatch*, regarding his experiences on the Alaska trek. For the *Ohio Conservation Bulletin*, he included: "One impressive thing was that Alaska, like everywhere else, not only has some excellent fishing spots, but also a great many mediocre ones, and that the same troubles of inducing fish to strike plagues the fisherman there as elsewhere."

He traveled throughout the state to talk about his Alaskan adventures. In a speech to the Wayne County Chapter of the Izaak Walton League in Wooster, Ohio, during the spring of 1948, Bob described the struggle of salmon as they reach their spawning destination. He also conveyed "[t]he size and profusion of berries, flowers, and vegetables in the lower part of Alaska are hard to believe [including] pea pods over nine inches in length, carrots that reached to the knees, and cabbage heads that would not fit into a wash tub." Bob drew some of the Alaska wildlife in charcoal, talking about their habits and characteristics. He also emphasized to the group "that the wildlife in Alaska were being depleted more rapidly than the animals were in our western states. A halt must soon be called on the large herds of animals in Alaska or they will also be decimated."

The grandeur of Alaska's landscape and its wildlife made an indelible impression on Hines, appealing to both the artist and the outdoorsman in him. Alaska would become one of Bob's favorite destinations.

The collaboration between Hines and Dufresne provided another noteworthy reward for Bob. The Countryman Press, which published the limited edition of *Alaska's Animals and Fishes*, also released *Fifty Years with Brush and Rifle*, Bill Schaldach's biography of Carl Rungius. A German émigré, Rungius trained as an artist in Europe, then traveled to the western hemisphere determined to paint the large game animals of Canada and the American west. Rungius captured the essence of his animal subjects as vividly as he did their native landscapes. While in New York City for a press run of *Alaska's Animals and Fishes*, Bob purchased a copy of the Rungius biography. Schaldach intervened, escorting Hines to Rungius's studio near Gramercy Park in New York City. The room had a tall ceiling, as in many older buildings. Hines noted that it seemed as though every inch of wall space was covered with paintings, drawings, or trophies. Shorter in stature than Hines and peering through narrow squinty eyes, Rungius showed Hines a painting of mountain sheep in progress. What impressed Bob was that the master painter, who was well into his seventies, asked Bob how he might improve the painting. "The man was still trying to learn when he was 70 some years of age. I think that's phenomenal," Hines recalled.

Rungius inscribed and signed Hines's copy of the book as did Schaldach. The inscription reads: "To a promising young wildlife artist, Bob Hines, with the best wishes of the artist, Carl Rungius and the author, William J. Schaldach. March 12, 1946."

Hines had little recollection of the remainder of the visit. Around 10 a.m., Rungius suggested that before the men went to lunch they should have an aperitif. Bob reminisced, "Now I was a virgin when it comes to Scotch. I have never tasted it, I hadn't even smelled it." As Hines began to feel tipsy, he attempted to hide his glass on a table cluttered with bottles and brushes. Rungius noted that Bob did not drink his scotch, and he admonished the younger man to finish it. That is about all that Bob remembered about the visit adding, "I got clobbered." Hines later said, "That was the first time I ever got drunk, but at least I have his signature in my book, and I think a great deal of it."

Dufresne's trust in Hines's artistic abilities, the critical success of *Alaska's Animals and Fishes*, and the opportunity to travel to Alaska would bolster Hines's confidence and experience as a wildlife artist. In 1947, Dufresne traveled to Columbus, presumably at Hines's invitation, to speak to the League of Ohio Sportsmen during their annual convention in the Deshler-Wallick Hotel. Unbeknownst to Hines, Frank Dufresne would continue to influence Bob's career.

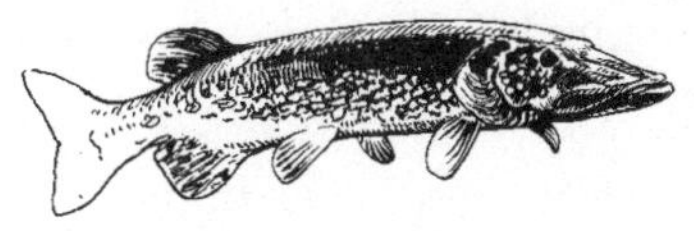

Chapter 5

The Art of Conservation

As Hines deepened his commitment to wildlife art, he expanded his network of contacts and developed his allegiances. In 1943, Hines signed a $100 one-year contract to create the cover artwork for *Pennsylvania Game News*. The November cover of the magazine stands out from the rest of his oeuvre because of its rare political statement. The image depicts an awkward wooden duck decoy with the impression of a swastika on its side and a sprig of aquatic vegetation draped across the loosely attached head, suggesting the frontal hairline similar to that worn by a notorious German leader at the time. A wave with turbulent white caps about to tumble back toward the imposter elevates the poorly disguised decoy symbolizing the rise of Adolf Hitler as three redhead ducks peer at it with anthropomorphized derision.

Following the warm reception for *Alaska's Animals and Fishes* in 1946, Hines accepted other freelance assignments. Charles Gillham, a grizzled, hard-drinking waterfowl biologist, recorded his experiences in Alaska and the Pacific Northwest with *Raw North*, a 1947 release from A. S. Barnes Company. Hines contributed his clean pen-and-ink drawings to that volume, as well as the chapter headings for *Outdoors Unlimited*, a collection of essays by Outdoor Writers Association of America (OWAA) members, which J. Hammond Brown edited, yet another 1947 Barnes release. Frank Dufresne was a coeditor for *Lure of the Open*, published in 1949, for which

Hines submitted a number of individual thumbnail portraits of the various wildlife species. Albert Day, director of the Fish and Wildlife Service (FWS), authored *North American Waterfowl,* also a 1949 release. Hines composed the illustrations for that book, which includes his depiction of the four major waterfowl flyways. Against an outline of the continent, innumerable tiny silhouettes of flying birds funnel southward, giving a visual aspect to these dynamic but abstract migration routes.

Representing the Ohio Division of Conservation and Natural Resources, Hines traveled to New York City in March 1946 to attend the Eleventh North American Wildlife Conference held in the Grand Ballroom of Hotel Pennsylvania. Bob had made his arrangements while back in Ohio, but when he arrived at the hotel, he was disturbed to learn that his reservation was invalid. Fortunately, Nash Buckingham, the dean of outdoor writing at that time, and Henry Davis were sharing a hotel room. They arranged to bring in a folding cot and invited Hines to stay with them. Buckingham had also participated in the OWAA trap shoot competition back in Vandalia the day Hines met Frank Dufresne for the first time. Remembering Hines's nearly clean sweep at the trap shoot event, the men had a laugh when Buckingham informed Bob, "You little squirt, [had I known] I wouldn't have shot off with you for all the tea in China."

Ira Gabrielson had agreed to speak at the conference, but he recently retired from the Fish and Wildlife Service to become president of the Wildlife Management Institute. Albert Day, the new Service director, spoke in Gabrielson's stead. Born in Nebraska but reared in Wyoming, Day had a brief stint as a signal corpsman in the US Army during World War I before he graduated with a bachelor of science degree from the University of Wyoming in 1922. Day went on to run rodent control for the state of Wyoming as part of the agricultural extension service. By 1928, his responsibilities expanded to include predator control. In 1937, Congress approved the Pittman Robertson Act, which levies a tax on firearms and ammunition, the proceeds of which are directed to the restoration of wildlife habitat. Ira Gabrielson, then director of the Bureau of Biological Survey, tapped Day to move to Washington, DC, to coordinate the administration of those funds. Before his retirement from the Service, Gabrielson wrote that Day "fully justified that selection by the fine job that he did in organizing the work and untangling the many new and knotty problems that arose." The outgoing director continued: "I have known him personally since 1921 and know him to be a capable public servant of the highest type. During the troublesome years through which we have just passed, I have given Mr. Day numerous difficult assignments and without exception he has handled them well. He is well liked by cooperators and respected by the numerous conservation organizations throughout the country. There is no doubt in my mind as to his ability to handle the work of the Service and I therefore earnestly recommend him as my successor."

Day had a strong commitment to the advancement of conservation on a national scale. His one shortcoming might have been his blunt manner of speaking, which he displayed at the Wildlife Conference. Day's talk was titled "The Problem of Increased Hunting Pressures on Wildlife." He began with:

> *In the years immediately ahead, the wild game of this country, not only waterfowl, but all other kinds as well, is going to face the greatest army of hunters in all history. The onslaught, in fact, has already begun. We felt the added pressure last fall when more duck stamps were sold than ever before. We're going to feel it a lot more next year. The push is on, and we might just as well brace ourselves to meet it.*
>
> *It is easy enough to figure out WHY the numbers of gunners and anglers have suddenly increased. Millions of our boys have now learned to use firearms. They have learned how to live in the out-of-doors, 70 per cent of the service men said they wanted to hunt; 62 per cent said they intended to go fishing. So do the homefolks. With new cars, new tires, plenty of gasoline, and with the war jobs all done, there is going to be more vacationing. America is going to move out into the open. Sportsmen are going to be searching out every bit of wild country they can find. Ducks, rabbits, bass, trout, and game administrators—look out!*

Day discussed the various factors that conspired against a surfeit of game for the approaching hunting season: a drought in the Midwest, increased hunting pressure on waterfowl over the past two years, and a declining population of target species during that same time. It appeared that tighter game laws, a shorter season, and reduced bag limits were in order. He then set aim on the organization Ducks Unlimited (DU). Day cited two recent publications both by S. Kip Farrington, Jr.: a book titled *The Ducks Came Back: The Story of Ducks Unlimited* and a *Reader's Digest* article, "The Quacker Comeback." Day conceded that DU was an earnest organization with admirable goals, but he said "many of us have long felt that the publicity agents for Ducks Unlimited have exceedingly active imaginations."

Quoting the *Reader's Digest* article, Day read: "The quackers owe their comeback to an organization called Ducks Unlimited, which since 1938 has boosted the continent's duck population by 500 per cent." Day chafed, "No mention is made either in the Digest article nor in Mr. Farrington's book of the waterfowl restoration program in the United States by the Fish and Wildlife Service with Duck Stamp or other funds—$20,000,000 worth—3½ million acres. The author does rather grudgingly attribute 'part of the credit to God.'"

Day pressed further:

> *He blames a liberal portion of the poor shooting in 1944 to his assertion that the birds were on the sanctuaries where the hunters could not reach them. He says the refuges are run with duck stamp money so they should be opened up for our returning servicemen to shoot in. The entire tenor of this book is that all anyone needs to do to have all the ducks he wants to shoot is to contribute to Ducks Unlimited. Come on, boys—step up! It's just like buying clay pigeons. There's nothing to it—to Hell with all restraint!*

He then arrived to the point of his contention:

> *Thus, we as honest officials charged with administering this resource under the terms of treaties with two other great countries, and under mandates from the Congress, are to be berated and held up to scorn if our findings run counter to Ducks Unlimited propaganda. That, ladies and gentlemen, I resent, as every thinking conservationist must also. Whether you agree with the federal regulations or not, there is no better way to tear apart the waterfowl program that has worked so well during the past 10 or 12 years. I agree with Ducks Unlimited*

> *propaganda in one respect. The waterfowl restoration program has been "the conservation miracle of the century." I say, however, that it has been accomplished by many agencies, many groups, aided liberally by the hand of God, and that Ducks Unlimited has contributed only its small share.*
>
> *I cite this example of publicity, not as an attack on Ducks Unlimited, but rather as an example of why we need sound, sane publicity, based on facts, not fiction, if we are to have the intelligent support of the hunting fraternity.*

Hines, who was in the audience during Day's impassioned speech, watched members of Ducks Unlimited rushing to the pay phones to report to their colleagues after Director Day concluded his remarks. Day's speech, along with Bob's gradual alignment with the FWS may have been the reason for a personal bias against Ducks Unlimited. Even though a promotion of Hines's artwork as a featured DU artist may have given him an edge in the lucrative commercial art market later in his career, Hines refused to consider such an arrangement.

After World War II concluded, Frank Dufresne along with the core of the Fish and Wildlife staff moved from their temporary office space in Chicago to Washington, DC. When artist Kay Howe resigned from the Department of Information office because of personal obligations, Dufresne informed Hines of the opening and encouraged his friend and colleague to move to the Washington area to join the federal government.

Edna Hines refused to leave the Columbus area. The children were enrolled at good schools, and she was actively involved with coaching the Corallines, a women's synchronized swimming team. Perhaps moving to a major metropolitan area offended her Midwestern sensibilities. Nevertheless, Bob and Edna agreed to an estrangement that lasted until her death. The separation was not entirely amicable. Edna did not encourage her children to contact their paternal relatives. Trips to Fremont to visit Vera and Howard Beatty did not include any time with George Hines, who lived in the same town. However, when Bobbie Hines, Bob's niece, was enrolled at Ohio State University, Edna did offer her a place to stay when Bobbie's dormitory was closed.

The *Ohio Conservation Bulletin* bid farewell to Hines in an editorial:

> *Our likeable and nationally famed artist, Bob Hines, has come into the reward due to him by reason of a decade of industrious application to his beloved art, based on his native talent. Having become one of the nation's ablest wildlife artists, it was inevitable that the higher up fellows would take him away from us. And so along came the US Fish and Wildlife Service and took him over to Washington as of July 16, to put the stamp of real art and reality into their publications. In this widened field our boy will earn a high niche in the art world.*
>
> *We feel some reflected glory in Bob's triumphs, because he came to us a decade ago as a raw novice, and leaves us as a top level professional—and we feel, as he has often assured us, that we helped him along in one way or another. Our best wishes and high expectations go with him.*
>
> *Bulletin readers who have come to take such interest in Hines' work, need not feel too badly about this because we have an arrangement whereby his work will continue to appear regularly in the magazine, and in Division miscellaneous publications. His interesting family will remain in Columbus.*

In an article titled "Two OWAA Boys Leave Ohio Home Fires" the *Outdoor Writers* newsletter informed its members that Hines had accepted a position with the Fish and Wildlife Service in Washington, DC. "If the old Chinese proverb that one picture is worth ten thousand words is true, it is hard to say how many millions of words Bob has equaled during his work out in Ohio and now all of his many friends will wish him an even greater career on the National level."

Bob Hines moved bag and baggage alone to the Washington area. His finances stretched as he continued to pay for the family house in Columbus, the education bills and routine living expenses for his children, and an apartment rental for himself in Arlington, Virginia. Bob's official position was visual presentation information specialist (Grade CAF-9) with a starting salary of $4,149.60 annually. At the time of his separation from the Ohio Division of Conservation and Natural Resources, his salary there was $3,650 per year. After Hines's departure from Ohio, he continued to contract with his former employer, composing "Under Ohio Skies" and completing artwork for the *Ohio Conservation Bulletin.* A 1949 issue of the *Bulletin* features a Hines rendering on its cover, an aerial view looking down at a mallard flock flying over manicured farm fields. The "Editorial Bulletin Board" reveals that the image is "Bob Hines' reaction to frequent airplane trips between Washington and Columbus." The editor offers the rhetorical question, "Doesn't this picture give you a sort of airborne feeling, with a tingling in your arms indicative of wings?" Ronald Karns, an aspiring young artist from Akron, sent the *Bulletin* his drawing of a sturdy eight-point buck. The editor printed the image along with the disclaimer, "Bob Hines came to us a decade ago just about as amateurish as Mr. Karns admits being—and look where Bob is now. Come in, Ronald, and we'll help all we can—we love to help young people to get started up the ladder." Replying from "Washingtonway," Hines graciously commented, "That deer head drawing by that young fellow who wants to make wildlife his work was exceptionally good, and it makes me all warm inside to think of the way that you have helped me, and will help this young man." The editor expounds further, "Bob is one of our boys, and there are others whose climb to success we have watched with keen interest and bask in the reflected glory on the theory that helping others to succeed is blood brother to doing those big things personally." Without a staff artist, the *Bulletin* included more photographs on its cover, often by Hines's former colleague Walter Lauffer. By late 1951, the Division hired Alvin Staffan as its next artist. Staffan's artwork was satisfactory, but his stiff, wooden poses lack the vitality of Hines's fluid style.

The first day of a new job can be an anxiety-provoking experience with its uncertainty and adjustments to a new routine. When Hines arrived at the Information Office at eight o'clock that morning of July 16, 1948, he was unprepared for a rebuke from his boss Frank Dufresne.

"Where have you been?" asked Dufresne.

Hines replied, "In Ohio, I started at eight a.m."

"That's not the way it is," Dufresne informed his new employee. "From now on you *will* be here at a quarter of eight."

Photographs of Hines from his early years at the Service show a handsome, slender man with a ready smile and a forthright gaze. As a reminder of an era predating business casual, he usually is attired in a dress shirt and necktie if not a sports jacket or suit. Later color photographs reveal a full head of sandy brown hair and pale blue eyes, the hue of washed denim.

Hines went to work pasting letters onto labels for a stack of pamphlets and assorted publications. As the new staff artist, he received the assignment to create the artwork for the covers of the *Pittman Robertson Quarterly*. His first piece for this project was a scratchboard of an ermine in its white winter coat; with a touch of subtle humor, the image includes the hindquarters of a mouse escaping the predator by diving into the surrounding snow.

Bob learned about the limitations of a government publishing office. For cost-cutting measures, the majority of the publications were printed in black and white. The powers that be were strict regarding the use of color in their printed materials. Color could be employed only to identify a particular subject, not solely for aesthetics. The cost of color printing could be up to five times that of the more economic black-and-white alternative. John Ady, a liaison between the Government Printing Office and the Service, took his job of cost cutting and budgets very seriously. Hines customarily signed each one of his completed pieces back at the Ohio Conservation Division. Ady told Bob in no uncertain terms that was not permissible; an artist's signature could be interpreted as self-promotion at the government's expense. Ady threatened Hines: Bob could lose his job if he continued to sign his artwork. Pushed to the brink of anger, Hines developed a way to incorporate his signature in the body of the piece so that deleting his name would destroy part of the composition. Remarkably, even Ady acquiesced to this tactic.

Hines grew weary with the routine of office duties; he envied those employees who had opportunities to travel. He expressed his dissatisfaction to Dufresne: "I persuaded the boss that I needed to see things if I was going to paint them." Dufresne made arrangements to take his new office charge to Pea Island off the North Carolina coast in January 1949. Dufresne's wife Klondy (her given name was Klondike after her birth in Nome, Alaska) went along to see a new part of the country. Hines enjoyed seeing otters, gadwalls, and his first greater snow geese. Incredulous, he commented, "Can you believe freshwater otters out in the ocean? That's what it amounted to." Another vivid memory was the number of peregrine falcons on that barrier island. Hines recalled: "It was the greatest concentration of peregrines I think I have ever seen." There were short telephone poles secured in the sand. Looking northward, Bob noticed a peregrine on every pole as far as he could see.

There was another revelation on that North Carolina trip. Bob's solitude in the lodge at Mattamuskeet National Wildlife Refuge was interrupted when Klondy and Frank Dufresne burst into the twelve-bed barrack in the midst of a pillow fight. "They had a room next to me down the hall just a little bit, and I was sitting there doing some kind of drawing. The door burst open. Frank comes running in, hollering like a banshee. He jumped from one bed to the other, and out again. Klondy's right behind him swinging a pillow, feathers flying all over the place. I heard a crash when they got over in the other room. They were laughing, having fun. Here they were 50 years old at the time. I think it's wonderful. They enjoyed each other."

After the Mattamuskeet trip, Hines was to paint a mural that showed the hunting blinds on the refuge. With Bob's talent and inspiration, the piece took on a new purpose. The composition of oil painting on wooden board teems with wildlife depicting some fifty species that reside on the refuge. The representations in full color are not mere portraits, but they convey the individual habits and attitudes of the various species. This was the first of Hines's efforts to become a muralist.

As the wanderlust continued to tempt Hines, Dufresne gave him another assignment—a seven-week trip to "the duck factory of the continent," the Delta Research Station outside Winnipeg, Canada. Bob would accompany the flyway biologists during the summer of 1949 for a cooperative effort between the Fish and Wildlife Service and its Canadian counterpart. The *Ohio Conservation Bulletin* reported, "Our boy, Bob Hines is happy. He's going to do the Northland with pencil and drawing pad. As he puts it: 'I have run into fate in a big way . . . imagine being sent to Manitoba, Saskatchewan, and Alberta to chase ducks around in government planes and chase 'em with government crews for banding. . . .' He's going soon, but is working ahead to provide Bulletin art."

After a few days of personal time with his family, Bob departed from Columbus to Winnipeg via Chicago, Minneapolis, Fargo, and Grand Forks. During Hines's oral history he recalled plans to "fly north to Hudson Bay at a great altitude of 35 to 50 feet to count every duck we could see." Biologist Art Hawkins was the team leader. Accustomed to this low-level flying, Bob began to fret when the airplane, an "old Seabee, one of the most disheartening craft ever flown," gained altitude to cross Riding Mountain in western Manitoba. Bill Arline, the pilot, had flown over The Hump several times during World War II. It did not help that the airplane, designed for two people and their gear, contained three men as well as a sack of two timber wolf pups determined to chew through their cloth enclosure as well as the pant legs of the men. Arline, according to Hines, with "just a little bit of a show off in him," landed on a lake in Ilford and shoved the propeller in reverse to stop it. However, the propeller did not obey, causing the plane to veer into a pile of logs, breaking a pontoon strut on the right wing. The pilot, with a measure of playful arrogance, blamed the accident on Hines who was sitting next to him. The men spent their July 4th chopping a cedar log to the size and dimension of the broken strut. Because of Bob's smaller hands, he had to secure the nuts within the plane's wing as Arline removed the bolts during the repair process. It was midnight by the time they reached Churchill. There were dark storm clouds forming against the midnight sun of the arctic; the airplane buzzed the landing strip to scatter the caribou gathered there. Hines recalled that members of the Canadian Air Force stationed there "came out, they knew we weren't going to be able to land such a clumsy looking airplane, but we did."

Ever observant, Bob located a four-leaf clover in the shadows of the grain elevator at Churchill. After departing Churchill, the team flew throughout northeastern Manitoba then westward to Winnipeg and Calgary. Bob wrote: "That was a flight! Navigation was entirely by map and compass and 'seat of your pants,' a six day food supply was a two pound ham and a few sandwiches, fuel was gas shipped ahead in barrels and laboriously pumped aboard by hand." Out on the muskeg, Arline flew over a huge wolf escaping the approach of the airplane. Bob continued: "[We] matched our wings against the legs of a giant white male, sending him into such a terrified flight that he threw spray higher than his head with every stride across the thawing land." Hines was enthralled, saying later "it was the most magnificent display of animal strength I had ever seen, you could see every muscle in his body." Bob earnestly tried to capture the image of the majestic canine in motion using an old Service camera. After Hines returned to Washington, he learned that the camera was faulty and that he had lost every image of the wolf. Hines became so upset with the revelation that he went to the restroom and promptly vomited.

The inside front panel of the September 1949 issue of the *Ohio Conservation Bulletin* features "Flying with the U.S. Biologists," an artistic synopsis of Bob's Canadian trip. The rendering documents that he was "Far enough north to see caribou. Far enough west to see pronghorn antelope." Hines later wrote another account of his adventure for the Audubon Society of the District of Columbia's periodical, the *Wood Thrush*. The piece is remarkable for his use of vivid imagery. He writes of the "spruce clad islands" where he heard "the hymn of the olive-back thrush;" of "male phalaropes hanging six feet over your head on the invisible ropes of the wind, calling, beseeching, urging you to leave their nearby eggs or chicks;" foxes with "tails so huge and feather-like they seemed suspended on hidden balloons;" "snowy owls that drifted like huge snowflakes over the tundra." Unfortunately, Hines never wrote another experiential essay of this caliber.

Frank Dufresne retired from the Service in 1950 to accept a position with *Field & Stream* magazine. He and wife Klondy moved to Olympia, Washington, where they lived in a bayside house on the water's edge with a panoramic view of the water. Dufresne wrote to Alastair Macbain, his successor in the Information Office at the Service, mentioning the five hundred or so birds of several waterfowl species visible from inside their home: "Tell all this to Bob because I can't help thinking what a grand setting for an outdoor artist is our front window with its enormous plate glass."

Macbain replied to his predecessor: "Bob Hines is still drooling as the result of your message," adding with friendly candor, "I'm afraid nobody here feels sorry for you."

Hines's duties with the Service were quite varied. He illustrated scores of Service publications; he traveled extensively drawing, photographing, assisting in wildlife surveys, and even scuba diving. He explained some of the activities for the book *Nature's Guardians: Your Career in Conservation*: "I do Old English and other types of lettering. I draw pictures of people and of fish, birds, and animals. I make technical drawings for scientific papers, prepare magazine layouts, and take a hand in arranging educational displays—none of which I could do if I didn't have a flair for wildlife work." Information chief Alastair MacBain supported Hines's bid for a promotion to Grade 11 by vouching: "Bob is one of the few people who can go to conferences, meetings, etc., and represent the Service adequately and without fear of violating any policies. Also, he is of considerable help in developing the story line and technical shooting script for motion pictures and, in addition, gives advice on Service activities which the motion pictures portray. In Bob Hines we are fortunate in having on our staff an employee who is recognized as one of the country's outstanding wildlife artists. The problem is to write a job description which sets out clearly his unusual duties and abilities."

After Dwight Eisenhower became president in 1953, he chose Douglas McKay as his Secretary of the Interior. McKay graduated from Oregon State College with a bachelor's degree in agriculture. However, he pursued a career in business, starting a Chevrolet dealership that later sold the Cadillac model as well. McKay ascended into politics in the Republican party, culminating in the Oregon governorship in 1948. He had an unassuming, plain-spoken Harry Truman quality to his personality, often referring to himself as "the old car peddler." With McKay's experience, he was a good fit in President Eisenhower's cabinet, which had solid ties to the business interests in the country.

Albert Day's commitment to the ideals of wildlife management on the federal level, along with his blunt manner, created friction with some prominent businessmen. McKay met privately with Day informing him that as Interior Secretary McKay wanted to appoint his own Service director. McKay chose John Farley to succeed Day. Farley received his teaching certificate from the Teacher's College in River Falls, Wisconsin. After teaching science at the high school level for four years, he enrolled at the University of Wisconsin to earn a bachelor's degree in electrical engineering. Farley's resume contains five years of experience as a sales engineer at Pacific Gas & Electric Company, then on to another five years in an administrative position with the California Fish and Game Commission. After a period of self-employment as a building contractor, his final employment was in the Public Relations Department for the Crown Zellerbach Corporation, a California-based pulp-and-paper manufacturer. Farley took a leave of absence from Crown Zellerbach to return to the US Army during World War II; he applied for another leave to enter public service as the newly appointed director for the Fish and Wildlife Service.

Rather than resign outright, Albert Day accepted a demotion with a pay cut to be one of three assistants to the director of the Fish and Wildlife Service, responsibilities he shared with Clarence Cottam and John Kask. Day held that position until 1955 when he retired from the Service to be the executive director for the Oregon Fish Commission. Alastair Macbain asked Hines if he might do a painting for their esteemed former director. Bob obtained a photograph of Day, which he admittedly traced to achieve the correct proportions. Hines then recorded anecdotes from Day's career in the Service. The final version depicts the caricature of Albert Day "mushing" away on a dog sled, surrounded by various mileposts from his career, one of which being when he raised the roof at the Hotel Pennsylvania in 1946.

There was such an impressive attendance at the official retirement event for Day that the festivities were held in the large Interior Department auditorium. At the unveiling of Hines's cartoon, Day, with a rotund build and a ruddy complexion, took one look at the piece and collapsed in paroxysms of laughter. His glee delayed the program for about fifteen minutes. Years later, Hines attended Albert Day's funeral in the Harrisburg, Pennsylvania, area. After the ceremony, Bob went to the family's home and recognized his retirement cartoon of Al displayed prominently on the living room wall.

Hines unwittingly created a new tradition in the Service with the retirement collages becoming a perennial project. He estimated that he had completed about eighty of these retirement cartoons: "The idea mushroomed, and for a while I did them in the office. I think [I did] six in seven weeks' time, then the boss says 'Break it off, no more.' So I did them at home. I'd charge anywhere from $30 to $50 for them. It wasn't money making, but it was fun. I have received letters from wives [and] from recipients themselves. I've had a number of free drinks and a couple of free meals because of them."

Upon its inception in 1938, the National Wildlife Federation created an annual tradition of a sheet of colorful conservation stamps with an accompanying album that educates members about natural history. The opportunity for a commission piqued Hines's curiosity in the early 1940s, but he never investigated any details with the organization. Late December 1955, Roger Tory Peterson wrote to Bob inquiring if he would compose two watercolors for a theme of "making homes for wildlife." Hines replied affirmatively, "I've never stopped wanting to paint some of [the stamps] so your suggestion about turning out two of them is a mighty happy one for me." The commission quickly escalated into seven paintings for a welcome payment of $655. Hines's beaver design is the image featured on the front cover of the Federation's 1957 album. Peterson continued to request watercolors from Hines for the next two years in the conservation stamp series.

The Interior building displays wall murals at the head of the corridors leading to the respective services or bureaus within the umbrella of the Department of Interior. Bob offered to paint four murals on canvas to be displayed on the walls of the corridor leading to the assistant secretary's office. In 1957, Hines received a letter from Robert Johnson, the acting director of the Bureau of Sport Fisheries and Wildlife stating:

> *Our Fish and Wildlife Incentive Awards Committee has considered your suggestion pertaining to the need for appropriate paintings depicting fish and wildlife in the main entrance to the office of the Assistant Secretary for Fish and Wildlife. It is the recommendation of the committee, with which we concur, that a cash award of $250 and a Certificate of Merit be given to you.*
>
> *You are commended for your interest and initiative in submitting the idea. We know that your satisfaction in the preparation of the art work will be tremendous and equaled only by the pleasure of the persons privileged to view the paintings when displayed. We are happy to see you win this award which is possible under the incentive awards program.*

Later that spring, Bob completed four large colorful canvas murals painted in oils—one a dynamic depiction of commercial tuna fishing; a more serene image of a solitary fly fisherman in a rushing mountain stream; a scene of two cub brown bears flanking their mother, which is standing upright on her hind legs before a salmon stream; and the aforementioned mallard duck flock arising from a wintery pond. Hines had yet another opportunity to create a more lasting legacy that to this day continues to promote the genre of wildlife art while advancing the aims of conservation throughout the entire country.

Chapter 6

Duck, Duck, Goose, Swan

After Bob Hines joined the Fish and Wildlife Service (FWS) in 1948, already a Duck Stamp artist himself, he was eager to observe the selection process for a new design. At that time, the Law Enforcement section handled matters related to the Duck Stamp. Jesse Thompson was the chief of the section with Rodney Gascoyne his assistant chief. Of the eight designs submitted for consideration that autumn, Thompson and Gascoyne were partial to an image of a blue-winged teal. The design was very similar to a photograph from a recent Ducks Unlimited (DU) publication. Because there was some tension between the FWS and DU over the interpretation of data and its dissemination to the general public, Director Al Day vetoed that particular selection. Hines later wrote: "there was no in-depth critique, no close examination, and little discussion, all of which struck me as a rather lackadaisical way of doing things." Gascoyne turned to his "attractive" secretary to ask her which entry she preferred. "Lacking any art training or any knowledge of waterfowl," she chose an image of two common goldeneye ducks in flight by Roger Preuss (pronounced *price*). That design appears on the 1949 stamp.

Hines was appalled at the casualness of the selection process. He turned to his chief, Frank Dufresne, and suggested a more formal contest with "rules, guidelines, and qualified judges." Director Albert Day agreed with a plan to transfer the open contest to the Information Office. Hines chaired a steering committee for the following year's stamp selection. A press release revealed, "An impartial judging committee will review all entries and select the design to be used on the new duck stamp. . . . The artists' names will be covered and the designs judged solely on their merits. . . . The subject . . . must be a true-to-life portrait of wild waterfowl. . . . [T]he birds should be in position and plumage 'as the hunter sees them.'" There were an abundant twenty-two judges for the first contest in 1949. Day and Dufresne assigned the regional directors for the Service, who were in the area for a meeting, to be judges. Day also recruited "Pink" Gutermuth of the Wildlife Management Institute, two US senators, and Earl Ohmer, chairman of the Alaska Game Commission, for the event.

Artist Walter Weber submitted a rendering of two trumpeter swans in flight over Red Rocks Lake in Montana. Hines acknowledged, "Trumpeter swans are not legally hunted, but they are residents on refuges where the Duck Stamp monies benefit." Weber used Payne's gray ink for his background; though a black ink, it has a bluish cast when diluted. Hines approved this use of a color wash when the judges approached him questioning the technique. Recalling Weber's design, Bob said, "His resulting drawing of these snow white swans against that dark blue sky was the best thing that anybody saw in that whole show."

The judges were instructed to score each entry numerically: three points for first place, two for second, and one for third. Weber's piece was well ahead by a spread of thirty points. His trumpeter swan design, released the following year in 1950, inaugurated the Duck Stamp contest. That first open competition was a success with the promise of more to follow. Meanwhile, Roger Preuss had a flair for self-promotion. When he released the second edition of his Duck Stamp print, Preuss gave the misleading impression that he was the first artist to win the contest. This fallacy irked Hines, who drafted a statement with his recollection of the events regarding the selection of Preuss's design. Bob reiterated there was no way that Preuss could have *won* the contest because there was no *contest* the year his design was selected.

The Service encouraged artists to strive for anatomical accuracy in their subjects. Service writer Edna Sater coordinated publicity and recorded the rules. Initially with submissions at a low number, photographer Emmett Haddon cut a series of 5"×7" rectangles in sheets of mat board to frame the individual pieces of artwork. He then hung these panels of multiple images on the wall for the judges to study. As the number of submissions increased, Bob fashioned sheets of plywood on wooden beams to display the entries. This arrangement worked fine until one year when the weight of the many drawings caused this new system to collapse, requiring an emergency call to the Interior Building maintenance crew. During the early decades of the contest, the number of entries averaged consistently around 150 pieces each year.

After Frank Dufresne retired in 1950, his successor, Alastair Macbain, encouraged publicity of the competition through his contacts with various publishers. By the following contest, the number of entries increased by 50 percent. Initially there was no limit regarding the number of entries an artist could submit. By 1954, the number received swelled to the point that Macbain suggested a way to shorten the judges' time. Hines's steering committee would cull those pieces with obvious anatomical or biologic errors, such as an Alaskan emperor goose flying over palm trees, or a drake redhead bringing sticks to a nest. (During an interview Bob explained, "Well, there's no sticks in a duck's nest, and drakes do not do anything around the nest.")

There were a number of questionable entries. One was a drake redhead duck with raised wings, "one wing was a natural looking feathered arm, the other just the bones with one single feather on the tip." Hines pondered, "We have never found what [the artist] was trying to tell us." One woman called to say she wanted to submit an owl drawing. Hines replied that she could, "but it wouldn't win because we weren't fostering owl hunters. She said something about 'stupid bureaucrats,' then hung up." Another woman called the office to inquire about the color of the drapes in the Interior Building auditorium, because she wanted to match the mat on her entry with the drapery. One unorthodox submission consisted of a piece of black linoleum divided into four sections, each the size of a standard 5"×7" entry. The "artist" then splashed white paint on each quadrant. Hines went to her application to verify her address; she resided at "some sort of institution." He added, "She must have had fun doing it, though."

During the 1952 contest, a twelve-year-old girl sent in her version of a duck dressed in hunting clothes and carrying a gun. That piece received national publicity, perhaps even more so than the selected design that year. The following year, artist and cartoonist Clay Seagers from New York sent in the winning entry of blue-winged teal. However, another Seagers entry created even more interest. Bob recalled, "It was a little derelict thing. The head was actually composed of a corn cob pipe inverted over the neck, and two mean-looking drake redheads were going to attack it." Clark Salyer, chief of Refuges, championed for that piece to be the final selection. While he was not successful, Salyer claimed he wanted to purchase the faux decoy painting for himself. Hines had high praise for the Seagers teal design, titled "Early Express," writing that "it captured the characteristics of the species as well as or better than any other stamp in the series."

At one point, the steering committee had to clarify the term *waterfowl* as strictly limited to ducks, geese, or swans because some entries featured such nongame birds as loons, grebes, and even whooping cranes. As the number of total submissions increased, there consistently averaged about twenty pieces each year that were the most eligible for consideration. This grouping became known as the "Top 20," separated apart from the other entries for closer consideration by the judges. In Bob's words, the "Top 20" pieces were the ones that "had the ingredients for a good stamp." Conversely, in Hines's files is a memo to Hines informing him that he "will have the function of screening out those entries that will not lend themselves to technical reproduction as a satisfactory design."

As coordinator of the Duck Stamp competition, Hines preferred that the panel of judges had an assortment of careers, training, and talents. From his experience "artists do a bad job. I can't explain [it]. We've had three instances where there were artists on the panel, and each time they kind of screwed it up. My own suggestion is that you take a guy who has actually lived in the marsh with ducks and geese, he's going to do a better job. My own invitation list would be guys who have served in the refuge system, on waterfowl refuges, or maybe they were poachers."

Bob specifically mentioned "Cigar" Daisey, the Chincoteague, Virginia, legend, a former poacher turned waterfowl carver. "He knows ducks like you wouldn't believe. He and I were judging a decoy carving contest, and we had a lot of fun, because he'd pick up a duck and look at its rear end and see if it's the right color back there, and he knew what color [it should be]." The personality of the judge was also a factor. "There [were] at least three cases in our judges where one guy was either loud spoken, overbearing, or maybe worthless, and he swung the opinion."

Roger Tory Peterson, himself an esteemed artist and author though never a judge for the competition, gave his unsolicited opinion of the quality of the Duck Stamps: "Not all choices have been of equal merit, which I suspect is due to the fact that most of the judges were not artists and may or may not have had a good sense of design or knowledge of what makes a good painting, or even whether the duck was drawn well. However, by and large, the choices have been good in spite of this difficulty."

Occasionally the judges would choose a final selection that featured a subtle flaw. John Ruthven's 1960 stamp depicts a pair of red head ducks and their four downy ducklings. Upon the selection of the design that year, Hines reminded Dr. Clarence Cottam, then assistant director of the Service, "drakes never help raise young ones." Cottam queried, "[W]hat are we going to do?" Bob replied, "You're not going to do anything, you've announced the winner. Then I told him that the ducklings didn't have wings, and he threw his hands up again."

Les Kouba's 1958 design of Canada geese had two shortcomings. First, the inspiration for the piece may have been a photograph of a captive goose because the wing feathers appeared clipped and did not fold across the rump. As Hines wrote to Kouba, "This goose has all the appearances of having its wings clipped, or maybe pinioned. The primaries of both wings are missing, and some of the secondaries and tertials of his right wing are not shown. One loose feather . . . is just long enough to make us wonder what is holding it in place." There was also an ear of corn in the foreground. Hines argued: "Now if we used that design exactly as drawn and submitted, we would have two violations of waterfowl laws. One of them was shooting or hunting over bait, which is what the corn is, the other is using live decoys." With permission from Kouba, Bob drew in the missing primary feathers; the Bureau of Engraving placed a bar bearing "US Department of Interior" over the ear of corn obscuring the other concern.

Hines was a stickler for accuracy. He would count the number of primary feathers on each entry, which should be ten on each wing. For the 1957 design, Jacob Miles Abbot portrayed nine primary feathers on one wing and eleven on the other of his common eiders in flight. Bob commented: "that would make a damn water-logged, misguided duck." He did not alter Abbot's original artwork, but Hines did correct the discrepancy on the photograph for the engravers. Similarly Ed Bierly's 1970 stamp depicts a preening Ross's goose extending its right wing in a straight line. With Hines's taxidermy training, he felt that the pose in reality was anatomically "absolutely impossible." Bierly also failed to add a wing on the opposite side of the bird. Again Hines drew in an opposing primary feather, the suggestion of a second wing on the photographic copy that went to the engravers. In good humor, Bierly sent an artist proof of his print to his colleague with the notation, "To Bob Hines, who has a primary interest in this painting." In all, Bob recalled eight instances where he silently corrected minor errors in the photographic proofs of the winning entries without changing the overall design of the artwork.

While Hines was the contact person for the competition, he was not involved in the other aspects of the Duck Stamp program, such as licensing, marketing, or the allocation of revenue generated from the sale of the stamps. If Bob was the engine behind the contest, then the public face belonged to his assistant, Bea Boone.

Beatrice Boone was born and educated in Massachusetts. She began her secretarial career in the Boston area earning an average of $25 per week. While working as a typist in the Boston Veterans Administration office, she transferred to the Washington, DC, Veterans Administration office in 1946. Two years later, she obtained a promotion with an opportunity to join the US Navy Department, obtaining a secret clearance to prepare statistical tables for naval publications. In 1951, she married Stephen Bialobreski, but maintained her more succinct maiden name because of her husband's unwieldy ethnic surname. After leaving government work, Bea went into the private sector. Her last such job working for an engineering company offered her little potential for growth. She then decided to return to the government payroll in 1967, applying for a position as a photolibrarian with the Office of Conservation Education in the Interior Building.

Initially, Bea worked for Bob Hines and two photographers, Rex Schmidt and Luther Goldman, whose office space was in the north penthouse of the Interior Building. Always interested in advancing her knowledge base to improve her job skills, she completed two classes in photography ostensibly to give her some insight into the photographers' craft. After Schmidt and Goldman left the Service (Hines maintained that they did so against their will), Bea became Bob's sole charge. Petite, scarcely five feet tall and one hundred pounds, and loquacious, she was the ideal interface with artists, judges, art dealers, and the media. Her personnel file is replete with letters of appreciation for her helpfulness and efficiency.

By 1969, Bea obtained a promotion to visual information specialist. Regarding the Duck Stamp contest, she would answer questions, record all of the entries received, send a letter acknowledging their receipt, return those pieces that did not comply with the guidelines, and return all original artwork at the conclusion of the competition. For judges, she would send invitations, handle travel arrangements, and reserve hotel rooms for those arriving from out of town. Hines recalled, "She began to take an almost scrappy attitude of protection toward the Duck Stamp [contest]. She was very aggressive in trying to be accurate, and anybody that didn't agree got told off. [I]t doesn't mean she was always right, but she was seldom wrong." Though childless, Bea would channel her parental instincts to protect Hines, who was living alone with no local family support system. Back at Bob's apartment, he might overextend himself by staying awake late at night with his freelance work, returning to the office early the following morning. Bea would filter his calls and appointments while he took power naps with his head and chest leaned against his drawing board. Once Clay Hardy visited the north penthouse office when Bea was away from her desk. He was surprised to find Hines lying on the office floor, sleeping off an "optical migraine."

The director of the FWS traditionally writes a letter of congratulations to the winner of each year's competition. Beginning with Ed Birely in 1955, the winning artist also received a full sheet of the official stamps during the following year's contest. Other than the sheet of stamps and the distinction of having a winning design, the top artist received no monetary award from the Service. The collector's art print market became a very lucrative outlet for the winning artist. As modern printing techniques improved, a design can readily be reproduced into thousands of copies. Hines groused to his friends that the monetary rewards were few when his design appeared on the 1946 stamp. In 1979, magazine writer Sam Iker referred to the Duck Stamp contest as "the world's richest art competition." Discussing Martin

Murk, whose design appears on the 1977 Federal Duck Stamp, Iker reveals: "Although the 'duck stamp contest,' as it is familiarly known, offers no cash prizes, it is probably the most lucrative art competition in the world. The winning artist gains immeasurable prestige; beyond that, he . . . can earn a bundle of cash selling signed and numbered prints of his entry. Some 5,800 such reproductions have grossed Marty Murk about $450,000—a sum four times as large as the Nobel Prize." As the potential for instant fortune spread among the wildlife art community, the number of entries escalated exponentially to a peak of around 2,100 in 1981, a workload that taxed even Bea Boone's organizational skills.

Heretofore, there was no limit to the number of entries one person could submit. Around that time, a request to place a registration fee of $15 won congressional approval, thereby discouraging nonprofessional entrants while at the same time curtailing the number of submissions. The revenue from the registration fees did help to defray the inherent costs of postage and travel and lodging expenses for the judges. The registration fee subsequently increased to $50, further limiting the number of entries per artist. In 2011, the registration fee was $125 per entry.

Hines recalled that while he was at the helm of the Duck Stamp contest his office never lost a single entry. There was one instance in which Mrs. Boone mailed two paintings in one envelope. However, the recipient recognized the mistake and returned the errant artwork, which in turn found its way back to its rightful owner. One year, the submissions were on display in the lobby of the Interior Building. Despite the presence of armed guards, one painting disappeared. Hines's boss, Dan Saults, wrote a letter of apology to the artist of the missing painting. Saults complimented him, stating that the piece must have been exceptional because the culprit took that particular painting and none of the others. His explanation must have appeased the artist because the issue did not proceed any further.

As the potential for financial gain swirled around each contest, there were grumblings that the selection process might be slanted toward a particular artist. This misconception festered until 1974 when a major controversy erupted. A source suggested that the contest was predetermined and the judges that year were influenced going into the selection process. The upbeat press release from the Service gives no indication of an impending crisis:

Wildlife artists call it the richest art competition in the country—and this year's Duck Stamp award went to a dummy.

No dummy, however, is James P. Fisher, an Oxford, PA, artist, whose watercolor of a weather-worn wooden decoy against a sky-scape of three flying canvasbacks was chosen from 268 entries in the annual Fish and Wildlife contest. While there is no official prize other than the artist's work being featured on the 1975 migratory waterfowl revenue stamp, the winner usually realizes about $100,000, which is not duck feed, through sales of signed prints to collectors.

The remarkable thing about the decoy choice was that it was not among the 20 final drawings submitted for the judge's consideration. However, two judges inspecting the 268 displayed entries noted the novel break with tradition and submitted the Fisher watercolor in the finals. Winning designs over the past 40 years have all featured live waterfowl.

Hines always remembered the feeling of euphoria he had when he learned that his redhead duck design would appear on the 1946 Duck Stamp. Bob insisted on personally contacting the winner of each Duck Stamp contest when possible so that he could instill that same sense of bliss in the artist. His intentions were blunted during the 1974 contest when James Fisher's agent, Freddie King, was in the audience. Hines was apoplectic when Bea Boone revealed to him that King was using Hines's office phone to contact Fisher about his winning design. Hines approached the man and told him in no uncertain terms that it was Hines's role to contact Fisher. This altercation was just a prelude of the controversy to follow.

The Interior Department coordinated an investigation into possible improprieties in the Duck Stamp contest, interviewing Hines, Bea Boone, Pete Anastasi, and everyone associated with the event. The anxiety was palpable during a hearing at the Russell Senate Office Building where the future of the Duck Stamp contest remained uncertain. The final agreement was that the competition would continue but with some modifications regarding "the qualifications and selection of the judging panel, the criteria used in scoring the various entries submitted, and the voting procedures to be employed by the judging panel." While the investigation found no evidence of wrongdoing and cleared the Duck Stamp contest and Hines of all charges, Bob never forgot those allegations that impugned his integrity.

Hines retired from the Service in 1981, but the Duck Stamp contest continued to evolve under the direction of Bob's good friend Pete Anastasi. The fraternity of Duck Stamp artists changed considerably in 1990, the fortieth anniversary of the Duck Stamp open contest, when Nancy Howe of East Dorset, Vermont, became the first woman to create a winning Duck Stamp design. Her acrylic rendering of a pair of king eiders was the top selection out of 626 entries. Interior Secretary Manuel Lujan called Howe in Vermont to hear her say, "Oh my goodness, that's incredible! I've entered the contest for a number of years[,] and I've been wondering when a woman would win." Howe revealed that she had entered her artwork about ten times in prior contests. She traveled to Washington with her husband and two young sons to meet with President George H. W. Bush the following afternoon at the invitation of Secretary Lujan. Around that time, entries by female artists comprised about 25 percent of the submissions. Even though women have placed in the top three designs in years past, as of 2011 Nancy Howe remains the only female artist to win the top honors.

During the 1990 contest, the Department of Interior Museum featured an exhibit of Bob Hines's artwork to salute "Mr. Duck Stamp Contest." Hines had been retired from the Service for nearly a decade. In 1988, the Smithsonian Museum of National History hosted "The Legacy Endures," a major exhibition of the Federal Duck Stamp program as well as waterfowl conservation. For this event, Bob completed two murals that identified "many of the waterfowl species and [located] the four principal North American flyways traveled by ducks and geese as they migrate up and down [the continent] each year."

Today Hines's brainchild, the Duck Stamp contest, the only federally funded art competition in the United States, continues to attract top-caliber artists. The Duck Stamp program in its entirety nets an average of $25 million of annual revenue that circulates back into the National Wildlife Refuges. Approximately 98 cents out of every dollar goes toward its stated goal of wildlife habitat acquisition and improvement, an efficiency rarely seen in many government programs. Since its inception in 1934, revenue from Duck Stamps has topped $750 million with the purchase of some 5.3 million acres of wildlife refuges. The contest has also enhanced the genre of wildlife art. When collectors purchase Duck Stamps, often in blocks of four, to accompany their art prints, the collector becomes an integral partner in the art of conservation.

To quote Hines: "[T]he revenues from the stamp sales are all for the birds—the restoration of waterfowl. It does not matter which of us, hunter or birdwatcher, will benefit the most. What does concern us is that wildlife artists and technicians are using their skills to maintain the high aims of this unique series—to keep the flocks flying. May the artists and the ducks both flourish."

Chapter 7

Journey to the Edge of the Sea

When Frank Dufresne called Bob Hines to inform him of an opening for an artist in the Fish and Wildlife Service's Information Office, Bob was less than enthusiastic to learn that his immediate superior would be a woman, a biologist named Rachel Carson. On impulse, Hines declined Dufresne's offer, stating later that "having done odd jobs for hard-to-please housewives during the Depression, I was apprehensive." Dufresne pressed on with the job offer, adding, "You'd better come because she is something different."

Carson was not in the office when Hines began working for the Service. He recalled sitting at his drawing board one day when "a slender, attractive lady walked in. She came directly to me, greeted me with a firm handclasp, and said, 'Welcome to the Fish and Wildlife Service. I'm Rachel Carson.'" It was a favorable first impression; Bob appreciated her direct manner. His office adjoined Carson's, which he remembered as "an uncluttered space with photos of a seascape and a large ghost crab." Hines learned to recognize Carson's approach by the sound of her heels tapping upon the terrazzo floors in the Interior Building.

As editor of the Service publications, Carson launched a series of twelve monographs titled *Conservation in Action*. Most of these featured one or more refuges in the National Wildlife Refuge system. Shirley Briggs and Katherine Howe, previous artists in the Information Office, had illustrated the initial volumes. Hines's first *Conservation in Action* assignment was to illustrate the monograph on Alabama's Wheeler refuge. Nine months after Bob began working for the federal government, he had instructions to assemble materials for an evaluation of his performance as a visual presentation specialist. He included a copy of the Wheeler refuge monograph with the following explanation of his responsibilities, which extend well beyond that of mere illustrations:

> *Wheeler, A National Wildlife Refuge was handed to me in complete manuscript form. To prepare it for proper and easy handling in the Government Printing Office, it was my duty to design, layout, prepare the dummy, select and prepare the illustrations, write the captions, specify the various type sizes and families, mark the drawings for proper reductions, and serve as the liaison man between the Fish and Wildlife Service and Mr. John Ady, Chief of Publications, Office of the Secretary, who deals directly with the G.P.O.*
>
> *At the time of this examination, I am preparing the material for two more pamphlets in this series, one for "Bear River Wildlife Refuge" and one on the Wildlife Cooperative Unit Program, both of which will include the same type of work as the enclosed.*
>
> *Without an extensive knowledge of wildlife in general, I am sure that I would never have received the several commendations I have gotten on this pamphlet, for several experts in waterfowl management have mentioned the accuracy of the illustrations and the selection of illustrative subjects.*
>
> *Mr. Frank Mortimer, Director of Topography and Design of the Government Printing Office, selected this pamphlet from among the thousands printed there to be placed on special display at the G.P.O.*

Carson coined the phrase "conservation in action" with this attractive and informative series of monographs. Bob assumed the duties of completing the artwork for five volumes. At Hines's own suggestion, he embarked on a project using the *Conservation in Action* title but executed in the same vein as his former "Under Ohio Skies" newspaper feature. Bob drafted a handful of undated proofs for distribution on a trial basis, but there is no evidence that venture met any measure of approval from the national media. The Service also owned a substantial collection of bird paintings by the legendary artist Louis Agassiz Fuertes. Bob catalogued the pieces at Carson's direction. With his artistic insight, he was able to enlighten her on Fuertes's style and technique.

While Hines was working in Ohio, Carson had written her first book, *Under the Sea-wind*, a 1941 release through Simon & Schuster. Unfortunately, the book appeared on the eve of Pearl Harbor and was all but forgotten during the ensuing war. At the time of Hines's employment with the Fish and Wildlife Service, Carson was researching what would become her landmark book about the world's oceans. Carson asked Bob to retrieve and deliver a number of books from several local libraries. As her network of contacts widened, Carson introduced Hines to her circle of colleagues. Avuncular Edwin Way Teale, who reviewed *Alaska's Animals and Fishes*, included in a letter to Hines, "I admire your work so much I would be happy to mention it to all the art editors I know. . . ."

Carson along with Marie Rodell, her literary agent, visited the Houghton Mifflin Company (HMC) office in New York City to meet with editor Paul Brooks in 1950. Both Carson and Brooks had an abiding interest in the natural world. Their conversation easily drifted to other book projects in development with HMC. Brooks must have mentioned that he was searching for an artist to illustrate a forthcoming volume on attracting backyard birds. Carson passed on Hines's name to Brooks, but a formal agreement needed the endorsement of Roger Tory Peterson, the art editor for HMC, publisher of Peterson's field guide series. Hines took a sample of his artwork, including the grayling and moose watercolors from *Alaska's Animals and Fishes*, which met Peterson's approval.

Brooks later wrote to Carson, "I don't know whether I ever thanked you adequately for putting me in touch with Bob Hines. Anyway, as I am sure he has told you, he has definitely taken the job of illustrating our *Picture Primer of Attracting Birds*, and I know that the results will be excellent."

Carson replied, "I was glad for everyone concerned that my suggestion on Bob Hines worked out. It is a pleasure to see his enthusiasm for the job."

Brooks had another project in mind that he discussed with Carson. He suggested an introduction to seashore life for the layman, an informative volume more like Peterson's *How to Know the Birds* rather than a true field guide. The idea resonated with Carson as she herself had thought about writing such a book. The discussion progressed toward its artistic format. In a subsequent letter to Carson, Brooks queried, "What do you think of your friend Bob Hines as a possible illustrator for the seashore book? I just received yesterday the bulk of his illustrations for *The Picture Primer of Attracting Birds*, and they are absolutely stunning. You did me a good turn when you put me in touch with him. Of course, this is all color work and I don't suppose that we are going to afford much color in the seashore book. However, his draftsmanship is very good, and I imagine he would also be effective in black and white."

Carson replied at length:

> *"Bob Hines would certainly be my own first choice as illustrator for the seashore book. I have delayed replying to your letter only because there still remained a possibility of a change in his work that might have made it impossible for him to consider taking on our book. However, I just talked with him, and I gather he would be open to a proposition from you. I am so glad to have your enthusiastic reaction to the paintings for* Attracting Birds. *I saw a good example of them and thought myself that he did an extremely fine job. Of course most of his work for us is in black-and-white, and I can testify that he is very effective there, too. From my standpoint, there would be great advantages to having him do the job. I feel that I shall have to work very closely with the artist if we are to achieve a completely happy result. Bob and I know each other so well that we already have a head start on this sort of teamwork. Then the fact that he will be, at least for the most part, here in Washington would make it easier. If he takes on the job I will want him to go to Maine with me this summer, and also to do some work on the southern sandy beaches and in Florida. I believe this would be necessary no matter who does the work, for we want a freshness of approach in the art as well as in the writing—no repetition of the museum type of marine art."*

Carson's book, *The Sea Around Us*, was about to appear in a serialized form in the *New Yorker* prior to the book's official 1951 release date. Hines recalled: "Rachel was a quiet woman. She told none of us at the Service when she sent her book . . . to a publisher. But one day she came to my office and motioned for me to follow her. She hurried to a public phone booth in the main corridor, pushed me inside, and crowded in to sit on my lap. She shut the door to ensure privacy and then told me that her book had been selected for the Book of the Month Club. Her eyes were large and wet and her laugh was almost a giggle—the only time I ever heard such a sound from her."

Within weeks, Brooks contacted Hines with an offer to illustrate Carson's next book: "I am happy to hear from Rachel Carson that you can illustrate her seashore book. She says that you 'would be open to a proposition' from us. Though this is not a job like the Picture Primers, where illustrations are the major feature of the book, I do feel that you should get some cut in royalty rather than the conventional outright illustrator's fee."

Brooks suggested an advance of $1,000 against a royalty of 2.5 percent of the book's retail price. He then went on a camping trip to the Great Smokey Mountains National Park. Upon his return, finding no reply from Hines, Brooks dictated another letter: "I'd hoped to find on my desk your okay on my suggested terms for illustrating Rachel Carson's seashore book. It would be nice to get this settled as soon as we can since—as she rightly says—author and illustrator should be working together from the beginning. I have just been reading the piece of her book on the ocean in the *New Yorker*. How that woman can write!" He concluded, "Russ Mason has presumably been badgering you by Western Union about the balance of the pictures for the Picture Primer and I imagine they will be en route by the time you get this letter, so I shall not badger you any further."

Curiously, it was Carson who responded to Brooks: "I know that Bob Hines had the impression that you were going to be out of the office for a couple of weeks and so did not hurry about replying to you. He has been laid up for a couple of days with a bad knee but I told him this morning that you were back and waiting to hear from him, and he said he would get something off at once." She added, "I know he feels he needs a little more information about the size of the job. . . . I do hope the thing may be worked out satisfactorily and soon for it will be a great advantage to have him go to Maine with me."

Prior to departing to the Upper Peninsula of Michigan for a meeting of the Outdoor Writers Association of America, Hines was preoccupied with his revisions of the illustrations for the *Picture Primer*. Brooks had earlier referred to Hines's artwork for the book as "magnificent." Hines concluded, "Aside from gaining rest after the illustrations are all in, I will also welcome that check, a little job of house painting to pay for." The correspondence between Hines and Brooks must have crossed in the mail; the latter contained a final payment of $500 for Hines.

Back in the Washington area, Bob wrote to Brooks, "Miss Carson has been having a hectic, but wonderful, existence, due to the earned success of her 'Sea' book. She intends to leave for New England within two days or less, and will probably go to Woods Hole first. I have just returned from a field trip to Escanaba, Michigan, plenty of sharptails, ruffed grouse, waxwings, et al [sic] to enjoy."

Lovell Thompson, head of HMC's trade division, referred to the duo of Carson and Hines as "a pretty high-class team." Brooks envisioned the seashore guide would be similar in shape to the Peterson field guide but slightly larger in size, "still small enough to go in the pocket or the picnic basket." By July 1951, Hines formally accepted the new contract from HMC, requesting a $1,000 advance for his travel plans. Around this time, writing from Woods Hole, Massachusetts, Rachel Carson relayed to Brooks that *The Sea Around Us* would appear on the *Times* best-seller list in fifth place: "Now if you can figure some way to take the army of would-be interviewers, feature writers, photographers, and the like off my neck, maybe I can get on with the "seashore book!"

Hines and Carson met that summer in Boothbay Harbor, Maine, residing on the east side of town in a cottage that Carson had rented. Bob later reminisced: "Rachel with her microscope and writing materials, I with sketch pads and pencils, and Rachel's mother, Maria, with her love of nature. We rented a seashore cottage just north of town with boulders stretching from the front porch to the ocean. It was here that my education in marine biology began." The project was a challenge to Hines as the invertebrates were subjects with which he was not familiar. He added, "I had difficulty with the scientific names, and in exasperation I called them all 'wee beasts.'" Bob's "Tidewater Sketch Book" documents quick sketches that evolve into more detailed portraits of the various marine creatures. There are also subtle touches of humor: an unfinished drawing of a crab with the caption "Darn! He moved!" A cartoon of pursed human lips expectorating droplets of liquid accompanies a study of sea squirts.

Hines began to understand Carson's strength of character. After Rachel collected an animal and Bob drew it, she insisted that the creature be returned to the same location from whence it came. "Rachel was adamant about this; her reverence for all living things—plant or animal—would accept no other way." Once while Carson was wading in a frigid tide pool at Pemaquid Point, her legs became so stiff that Hines had to carry her out of the barnacle-encrusted pool. "One cloudy day even her determination failed, and when she started to climb out of a pool, she was so numb she nearly fell back in. I splashed in beside her, picked her up, and carried her to the car. Mrs. Carson wrapped her in a blanket and asked me to drive home."

Bob respected the bond between Rachel and her mother, but occasionally he would tire of Maria Carson's romantic, childlike view of nature. A family of skunks resided under the porch of their rental cottage. Hines wanted to photograph the skunks, but Maria Carson was concerned that the camera's flash would frighten them. Hines explained that lightning did not deter the animals, but Maria remained resolute in her opinion. The last day of Bob's sojourn in Maine was overcast. While he was walking back to the cottage he spied the neighbor's German shepherd drunkenly careening into the bushes. "[T]he skunks had come out early [because of the dark sky] and the dog had come to see them. They met, much to the dog's sorrow. He got the full charge, and the poor old boy was half blind from the squirt."

Carson continued to juggle her job responsibilities at the Service with the pressures of a literary celebrity. In a letter to Brooks, she revealed that Hines's work on the seashore book was interrupted when he was admitted to the hospital for a tonsillectomy, his recovery further delayed by a severe reaction to penicillin. In 1952, HMC released *Mason's A Picture Primer of Attracting Birds*, a slender volume with Hines's lavish color plates. One reviewer commented, "the illustrations by Bob Hines are unusually colorful and exciting." The final version of the *Picture Primer* has a typographic error in which the key for the section "A Score and More Shrubs" has one entry duplicated, thereby disrupting the numbers for the remaining list of food-bearing shrubs that encompasses two pages. There is an insert of the errata clarifying the captions. Hines never spoke favorably about the *Picture Primer* in part because of that error: "The book was a failure. They printed 25,000 copies and I think they threw about 30,000 of them away." Bob felt that the book did not sell, not because of its printing error, but because of its steep price of $2.50.

Rachel had requested a leave of absence from her employment at the Service allowing her to travel and research her forthcoming book. As she made her way along the beaches of the southern states during the spring of 1952, Carson planned to meet Hines in the Florida Keys, where he was to be on assignment documenting the endangered Key deer. Traveling with his colleague, photographer Rex Schmidt, the two men could not locate the diminutive deer in its native habitat. The men decided to end their day with a movie at the local theater. To their surprise, Hines and Schmidt found two of the miniature deer gamboling on the manicured lawn of the theater. Hines overlapped his Service assignment with an opportunity to work with Carson in this habitat of mangroves and coral coastline. During their time together on the Keys, Rachel confided to Bob that she had decided to resign from her position in the Fish and Wildlife Service.

Carson struggled with adapting her lyrical writing style to accomplish an overview of the principal tidal creatures along the Atlantic shore. Lovell Thompson reminded Brooks, "I have encouraged [Carson] all along to let the book develop as she sees it. It is obviously going to be a more important—and a more literary—book then we originally envisaged, and I doubt whether *Seashore Guide* will be the right title for it. Rachel and Bob know each other so well that I think we can trust them to work this out together almost as if they were one author. We should probably be putting too much of a straight jacket on Carson–Hines if we tried to make them conform [to a field guide format]."

By that summer, Bob joined Rachel and her mother on Cape Cod, based at Woods Hole's Marine Biological Laboratory. Prior to his arrival on the Cape, Carson wrote to Hines: "I really think you should just plan now to stay two weeks. There will never, in the time we are working on this book, be another such opportunity, and I am most anxious to see you make the most of it."

Of their time at Woods Hole, Bob later wrote: "Twice we went out after dark to a world vastly different than it appeared during the day. The beams of our flashlights showed crabs of all sizes, feeding with a freedom unknown in the sunlight. Small fish came up close and were pinned in the glare of our torches. The sea walnut, a comb jelly with a glasslike body too fragile to be netted, was easily guided into open mouthed jars."

After traveling to Woods Hole for a meeting with both Carson and Hines, Brooks declared "the sample pages on the periwinkles strike exactly the right note."

Privately Rachel vented to Marie Rodell: "There is also the problem of Bob, who presumably is set to work on the thing all winter, but who does not take one step unless I am behind him with a sharp needle. I am delighted with the way he is doing the drawings and cannot imagine anyone else who would do them as well; but believe me, it gets done by the sweat of my brow as well as his."

Back in the Washington area, Bob informed Brooks "Have been working with the experts at the National Museum on seashore material, filling in some of the gaps in the field work, and am confident that the drawings submitted will be among my best." Brooks's cordial reply reveals his trust in Hines's artistic abilities: "Judging from what I've seen so far, I certainly share your confidence that this is going to be your very best work—which is saying a good deal."

As Carson began to develop a theme that would tie together the life histories of the various seashore inhabitants, she submitted her first draft to editor Brooks by early 1953. He agreed, "*The Edge of the Sea* is a good title [for the book]."

Meanwhile, Hines's efforts suffered a setback. He did not apply enough spray fixative to his first set of pencil drawings. They arrived smudged at HMC and needed to be redrawn. Recovering from the flu, Hines typed a letter to HMC. In his usual relaxed, understated manner, he concluded, "Miss Carson and I are hard at it, trying to put together a book of which we can all be a little proud."

B. C. Tilghman of HMC replied, “I have an idea that this will be a book of which you can be more than a little proud.”

Brooks began to express his concerns about the pace of Hines’s efforts. As an artist, Hines tended to view a deadline in relative terms rather than as an absolute endpoint. Brooks shared in a letter to Carson, “I think he’s doing a wonderful job and the only thing that keeps me awake at nights is the feeling that he might not meet the same deadline that I know you are going to meet with the text.”

Other than the stated cash advance of $1,000, HMC offered Bob no reimbursement for art supplies or travel expenses. He could claim those as deductions on his income tax, but that did not help with his cash flow. Moreover, Hines had recently purchased his first house in Columbus. His personal finances were further strained as he endeavored to cover mortgage payments, his own apartment rent, as well as the usual custodian care of his wife and two children back in Ohio. Bob accepted other freelance work that augmented his government salary.

Carson’s reply to Brooks was candid yet measured: “It is an odd coincidence that you happened to mention the problem of Bob, because I was lying awake last night thinking about it, and planning to write you in confidence to see whether we could work out a benevolent plot. It has really been a source of worry to me, for I’m certain he won’t finish anywhere near our deadline as things are. Heaven knows, I’m a poor one to complain, for I’m so far behind myself, but at least I am in that state of desperate determination that—judging by the past—is likely to bring me through about on time. About Bob—I understand his problem, having been through financial troubles myself, and I’m sure he keeps putting this off in favor of the small jobs that will bring him money now. In my less charitable moments, I resent his not finding some way out of the predicament; in kinder moods, I feel sympathetic, but the trouble is that neither attitude is getting results, and I think something will have to be done now, instead of just drifting closer to the deadline.” Carson suggested additional monetary advances as Hines completed the artwork for different sections of the book. She concluded, “I really feel that something must be done, and the only alternative to this that I can think of is the very unpleasant and undesirable one of an ultimatum to produce results or withdraw. Apart from the fact that we both like his pictures very much, it seems unthinkably difficult to begin all over with someone else at this stage."

Brooks turned to Marie Rodell, Carson's literary agent, for her take on "any more efficient methods based on [her] long experience with the recalcitrant artistic temperament."

Rodell, whose keen judgment could recognize the root cause of a dilemma, wrote back to Brooks, "I know of no better goad for an artist's temperament than cold cash."

Reflecting on Roger Tory Peterson's progression to a self-sustained artist, Brooks later intimated to Rodell that Hines might consider leaving the Service: "What I did have in mind . . . was our experience with Roger Peterson, whom we encouraged to give up his job at the Audubon Society . . . and take a chance on making a living out of royalties on his books. Since we had several book projects in mind, this seemed a fair gamble, and he certainly never regretted it. Of course he has done other short jobs . . . which have helped to fill out his income. But now—twenty years after the first publication of the *Field Guide*—he really no longer needs them."

Empowered, Brooks corresponded with Hines, "I realize what a big job this is and for that reason I think it would be a fatal mistake to postpone the bulk of it until the last possible minute. The drawings you have shown us so far are superb, but they represent only a very small proportion of the whole. Obviously we must find some way to make the work go faster." Brooks then offered Hines a plan of cash advances against his contracted royalty: $250 at the completion of the rocky shore section, $250 for the coral coast section, and $500 on completion of the entire assignment by July 1, 1953. Brooks added: "I needn't point out to you the importance of this matter to both of us. We have, in my opinion, the best possible illustrator for Rachel's book. You have an opportunity that any illustrator in the world would give his eyeteeth for."

On St. Patrick's Day, Hines replied to Brooks, "you have analyzed the financial aspects quite accurately. Existence has become a problem that the pay from my federal job does not cover well enough, and I have had to feed the kitty with freelance funds. Since author and publisher are both already well established as tops in their fields, and the artist cannot say as much for himself, it seems to me that the published results can mean more for said artist than for anyone else. And since I am said artist, I am and will continue doing my best."

Hines completed the rocky coast section by early May, for which Brooks sent him his promised royalty check. However, another period of creative stagnation ensued with Carson's writing. She shared with Hines during the summer of 1953, "You can now rest happy in the knowledge that I am now the chief bottle-neck in this project, and by the look of things will continue to be for some time!"

Meanwhile Hines shared with Brooks, "I was with my family last weekend—had a wonderful time chasing butterflies, which the kids and I identified with the aid of the *Guide* you gave me."

Bob's personal finances continued to trouble him. Writing to Brooks, Hines shared: "I have spent considerable time drawing and researching on this work, cutting off some of the usual smaller sales that have kept my economy afloat, to the extent that a particularly awkward situation has developed here. . . . I would certainly appreciate receiving another advance against royalties of $250. The problem arose because State Conservation agencies, for whom I turn out the odd drawing or two, have too many channels to go through before paying, meaning that such funds would be too late."

By March 1954, Carson remained doubtful of a fall publication date. The sand and coral chapters were coming together by that spring, with manuscripts and drawings submitted to the production department for layout. Around this same time, through Marie Rodell's intervention, editor William Shawn expressed an interest in printing an excerpt of the text with a handful of Hines's illustrations in the *New Yorker*.

As Carson shouldered the onus of polishing her manuscript and reviewing the galley proofs, Hines received a welcome diversion, an assignment from the Service to return to Alaska. His itinerary would begin on August 30 with a flight far from the edge of the sea to Missoula, Montana, by way of Minneapolis. Bob was to visit the National Bison Range complex including the adjacent affiliated refuges of Ninepipe and Pablo. Departing Missoula by Northwest Greyhound bus for Helena, he then traveled by train from Great Falls, Montana, to Minot, North Dakota. Hines recorded in his travel log book a personal expense of $4.70, a considerable expense at that time, for a long-distance call from Minot to Carson in Boothbay Harbor, Maine. During that conversation, he shared that prior to his departure an eye ulcer further delayed progress on his illustrations for the seashore book.

Beginning at the Lower Souris refuge (now J. Clark Salyer National Wildlife Refuge), Hines visited the refuges of Des Lacs along with Lostwood, all in the northern tier of the state. Departing Minot, he flew in a Service airplane to Edmonton, Alberta, and then onto Grande Prairie, where inclement weather, rain, and a low ceiling hampered his travel plans. When the weather cooperated, Hines departed Grande Prairie for Watson Lake in the Yukon Territory where he lodged with members of the Royal Air Force. From Canada he flew to Juneau, Alaska, reporting to the Regional Office (RO) there. After a series of meetings at the Juneau RO, Bob departed for Fairbanks by way of Skagway and Tok Junction, then on to Anchorage. From there, he stayed seventeen days in Cold Bay then was off to Kenai for two weeks. Hines left Alaska on November 9, arriving in Chicago the following morning. He concluded his trip with some family time in Columbus for a total travel time of ten weeks, all at the expense of the Service.

John Ball, the chief pilot for the Service, flew Hines into Alaska in the government airplane. "Flying cheek to jowl against the pilot," Bob recalled, "The Piper Pacer . . . was so small that when he breathed in, I breathed out. I mean we were that close. We had an altimeter, a gas gauge, a radio, I think that's all. The rest he did by the seat of his pants. We flew the Al-Can highway, because that would make an emergency landing strip." Hines continued: "The flying [was] fine, except when updrafts, downdrafts, and sidedrafts in the White Pass between Juneau and Whitehorse knocked us about a bit. The radio came loose, and I dented the top of the plane with my skull, but it was a valuable lesson. After seeing that little hunk of metal tubing and fabric survive that tossing, everything was an anticlimax, and my stomach never again failed me."

From that point, legendary pilot Clarence Rhode transported Hines throughout the territory with Bob in the copilot's seat. Hines described the event: "Then there was Clarence Rhode, the Old Man himself, as his men call him, flying a twin engine Beechcraft, showing me the white sheep in the Alaska Range . . . and the caribou beyond, pointing out the flocks of ptarmigan. . . . All the while laughing and joking and enjoying life, for that is definitely his way; rolling the plane sideways so that I could see the brown bears, mothers and cubs and solitary boars; sliding over the mudflats to put the emperor and snow geese into flight so that I could say I'd seen them. A million dollar experience, and being paid for it, that was all mine."

In Hines's files is a photograph of Ball and Rhode taken at King Salmon, Alaska, with Hines's handwritten notation: "There is an air strip at King Salmon—but the nite [sic] before this photo was taken, there was such a wind we almost tipped over trying for the runway and used the riverbank instead to form a lee while landing on the water." Rhode, the regional director for the Service in Alaska, was also an accomplished pilot. In August 1958, Rhode piloted a Service twin engine Grumman Goose airplane accompanied by his son and a fellow Fish and Wildlife Service agent. The aircraft departed from Fairbanks on a routine flight into the arctic reaches of Alaska then disappeared. Two hikers at the eastern aspect of the Brooks mountain range solved the mystery twenty-one years later when they spied remnants of the plane's wreckage at an altitude of nearly 5,700 feet.

For the prolonged duration of Hines's Alaskan adventure, there is no documentation in his federal file. He did revel in shooting his first emperor goose at Bristol Bay. Bob especially enjoyed the time he spent with Bob "Sea Otter" Jones, seventeen days with relentless fog and drizzle in Cold Bay, Alaska, at the far west aspect of the peninsula that gives way to the strand of Aleutian Islands. Hines reported: "And then I went to Cold Bay, where the wind blows free enough to scalp the tundra and the rocks of their coats of moss." Jones was the first refuge manager of the Aleutian Islands National Wildlife Refuge. He lived a hermit's life at Cold Bay, living off that barren land.

Hines reminisced, "There wasn't any grocery store there, we ate what we got with a shotgun or caught with a fly rod. I would bring the ducks and geese home and make drawings of them in the building there, and then we'd eat them." He continued, "We walked in the bear trails. We saw caribou, bears, and foxes, we saw hundreds of thousands of ducks, geese, and swans there for the fall migration. It was the greatest 17 days of my life."

On the eve of Hines's departure from Cold Bay, Jones wanted to collect some scaup for the RO in Anchorage. He and Bob shot several of the ducks, which drifted off to the side of a small pothole. As Jones walked around the water, he called to Hines, "On the far side in the snow were the beds of two Alaskan brown bears still steaming. They had taken off at the sound of our guns, and they were completely out of sight by the time I got there." The men took turns urinating outdoors around Jones's cabin, thereby creating a screen of human scent to deter the bears.

Hines typed a letter to Rachel Carson from Kenai in which he describes his impressions of the area and its wildlife. A highlight of that trip was at Cold Bay where he watched a trio of gyrfalcons—one of each color phase of that mighty arctic raptor—mob a group of ravens on a seaside bluff. "Almost as long as I have been able to read and dream, I have dreamt of seeing a gyrfalcon," he reported. "From now on I believe all birds will just be ordinary birds, for there is only one gyrfalcon. I have seen them, and I remember them, and I will always judge other birds by them." With a touch of his carefree humor, Bob added "[T]here may even be a [photograph] of your illustrator with a beard. Ho! It wasn't big and it didn't live long, but it was all itch!" Considering Carson's reserved personality, it is remarkable that Hines signed the letter "Love, Bob." Carson circulated the letter among her closest friends for their reading pleasure.

Returning home, Bob completed the finishing touches on a stack of the drawings for the book. By early March of 1955, after a visit with his family in Columbus, Hines contracted a severe cold that reduced his productivity; he reported that he discarded about 75 percent of the drawings he attempted during that illness. As Carson completed her manuscript, she queried Brooks about giving due credit to Hines: "I hope you are going to give some information on the jacket about the artist as well as the author. Apart from the fact that we share the hope that good things will come to Bob as a result of this, it seems to me demanded by the fact that the art is such a substantial part of the book, and is so beautifully and satisfyingly done." That August brought the serialization of *The Edge of the Sea* in two installments of the *New Yorker*. Editor William Shawn had chosen to include a few of Hines's illustrations, which provided Bob a tidy royalty.

As the publication date for *The Edge of the Sea* neared, Bob took it upon himself to design a special book plate. It depicts a tern in flight over water with a lighthouse along the shore in the background. Eager to please both Carson and Rodell, he shared the compressed schedule with Brooks: "I have special delivered the drawing for the autograph plate to Marie Rodell, who will rush it to Rachel Carson, who will rush it to you." Rodell was brutally frank in her assessment of Bob's design, "The mountain has labored and brought forth a microscopic mouse. In other words, here is Bob's sketch for the book plate and I don't see how it could be drearier or more commonplace." Thus, Hines's quest for the book plate met an abrupt end.

Paul Brooks arranged a party to honor both Carson and Hines at New York City's Club 21 in October 1955 prior to the official release of *The Edge of the Sea*. Brooks extended special invitations to Alastair MacBain, Bob's supervisor at the Service, as well as to Al Day, former director of the Service. In his reply to Brooks, MacBain graciously acknowledged not only the invitation but also an advance copy of the book: "I appreciate your invitation to the MacBains to help celebrate publication of *The Edge of the Sea*. Rachel Carson and Bob Hines are two of my favorite people. Please accept my thanks for the copy of the book. It is beautiful—in all ways. You, as well as the author and artist, are due congratulations." Hines greatly appreciated Brooks's gesture of including his Service colleagues in the evening's festivities. After the event, Bob wrote to Brooks: "I certainly feel that no artist ever had his work treated in better fashion than the way you and your staff have handled my part of *The Edge of the Sea*."

The book was Hines's greatest commercial success. *The Edge of the Sea* climbed to second place on the *New York Times* best-seller list, just behind Anne Morrow Lindbergh's *Gift from the Sea*. *The Edge of the Sea* remained on the *Times* best-seller list for twenty-three weeks. The success of the book after its prolonged and at times uncertain gestation was a boost to Hines's self-confidence and ego. That fall, Bob shared with Rachel: "[T]he encouragement you have given me by the way you accepted my work, and the way it looks when coupled with your writing, some . . . new source of energy and determination about work and life in general have created and maintained a fine feeling inside. I hope it shows in the way I treat people and in the way I work."

The collaboration of Carson and Hines became an intersection of two remarkable talents. Carson felt that her forte as a writer was to interpret science for the benefit of the laity. Hines pursued wildlife art as a means of educating the general public. Bob's exquisite pencil drawings reveal his deft draftsmanship, beautifully complementing Carson's lyrical prose. Zoologist N. J. Berrill adroitly articulated this partnership in his review of *The Edge of the Sea*: "Bob Hines' delicate and artistic (but always realistic) sketches are on almost every page, and they are curiously interwoven with the text in such a way that you cannot read the one without simultaneously seeing the other. As a result, the double impact is much stronger than if the two impressions came separately, and so *The Edge of the Sea* becomes the product of two naturalists working in close cooperation, each one scientifically trained and each an artist, the one with a pen and the other with a pencil. Together they take us on a good journey."

Carson likewise commented on the seamless marriage of the illustrations and print in a letter to HMC: "The book is really a beautiful thing, and both Bob and I are so grateful to you. The illustrations seem to fall so naturally, at just the right places, but (just as with writing that seems to flow with simplicity and grace) I can understand the painstaking effort and the creative skill with which you achieved such an effect. And I do not see how there could have been a better choice of type—nothing could have blended more harmoniously with the illustrations and at the same time be so pleasant to read." Hines achieved a degree of literary immortality by illustrating Carson's third book. Nearly sixty years after its release, *The Edge of the Sea* has never been reprinted without Hines's accompanying artwork.

The correspondence between Carson and Hines during their partnership on *The Edge of the Sea* suggests an informal camaraderie. Rachel encouraged Bob to consider an agent to handle his business arrangements for future projects. He took her advice and enlisted Marie Rodell, Carson's literary agent, as his advocate. After the financial rewards from the success of *The Sea Around Us* allowed Carson to construct a cottage at the water's edge on Maine's Southport Island, she christened her haven "Silverledges." Hines sent Carson a letter suggesting other names for her to consider, each a playful use of alliteration building on invertebrates that appear in his drawings.

Bob recalls that he spoke with Rachel by telephone after the publication of *The Edge of the Sea*, but there is little meaningful correspondence between them for several years. In one of his chatty letters, Hines reveals to Carson: "I have a reservation, arranged by J. Clark S[alyer], for the big log cabin at Seney Refuge, in Northern Michigan for 10 days the first week in September. The whole family, plus one neighbor boy, plus our pet woodchuck, is going to invade the area in search of perch, pike, butterflies, and whatever we can see. Since the kids have never seen live, wild deer, otter, bears, porkies [porcupines], or beavers, they will likely have a field day. PS, their father will enjoy it too."

Carson turned her attention from marine biology to the effects of chemical pesticides on the natural world. Late in 1960, Rachel learned that she had developed breast cancer. The following year, she began radiation treatments that sapped her strength. During the summer of 1961, Rachel asked Bob to drive her to her summer cottage on the coast of Maine. He later recalled: "We left her Silver Spring, Maryland, home around 8:30 in the morning. Rachel sat beside me; her eight year old nephew, Roger, and her black cat, Jeffie, were in the back. She was eager to get to her cottage in Maine where many of the frustrations of recent months could be forgotten. As we drove north, she seemed happy, but somewhere around New Jersey her talk turned grim as she turned to the subject of insecticides."

Carson continued, "[W]hen the facts are known, the chemical companies and very likely farmers and agriculture experts will deny most of them. . . . I only hope I'm strong enough to meet their charges, for goodness knows I have the data to prove the truth." After Hines delivered Carson and Roger to their destination in Maine, Bob photographed Rachel on the back deck of her cottage overlooking the Sheepscot River. From that photo, Hines later drew an undated portrait of Carson, which was discovered in his personal effects after his own death.

As Carson's last book, *Silent Spring*, neared its release in 1962, editor Paul Brooks never considered Hines to illustrate it. Perhaps Brooks held a bias against Hines for what Brooks perceived was inertia on Hines's part during the creation of *The Edge of the Sea*. Years later in a message on an undated Christmas card, Hines shared with a friend that after a visit with Brooks, "all business differences he and I have had in the past seem to be ignored."

The publication of *Silent Spring* incited an intense public debate with a faction of the agrichemical industry attempting to discredit Carson. By the summer of 1963, Rachel needed to return to her touchstone on Southport Island to rejuvenate her bruised psyche and failing physical health. Jeanne Davis, Carson's secretary, drove her and Roger to Maine in June; however, because of family obligations, Davis could not return at the close of summer to return them back to Maryland. Carson wrote a long-hand letter to Hines thanking him for copies of his new waterfowl primer, *Ducks at a Distance*: "I am delighted to have the generous supply of the waterfowl bulletin, and I trust it will bring the artist and creator more of the renown he so greatly deserves. No doubt you wish, as I do, that the color had been better—but then we old perfectionists shouldn't be so fussy." She continued, "Bob, I want to ask you something very tentatively—and I will do so only if you promise you will feel entirely free to say 'No, I couldn't do it.'" After inquiring if Hines would chauffer Carson and Roger back home to Maryland, Rachel added: "The reason I may have to break away early has to do with medical treatment, and I hope it can be put off until September. I don't know how much, if any, of the story I've told you—but whatever you know or think you know, please keep it carefully under that hat you never wear! This is one of those things I don't talk about, especially with news mongers hiding under every bush."

Carson concluded her last visit to her beloved Maine cottage in September 1963. Hines sensed her obvious physical pain and drove back directly to Maryland. Bob later recalled: "But as her fame grew, her health faltered. She was confined to bed and a wheelchair. I spoke to her once more by telephone. Her voice was slurred, and she assured me that she was not drunk, but under sedation. . . . I told her I loved her and that the whole world was waiting for her to recover." Carson died at fifty-six years of age in April 1964. Her family asked Bob to be a pall bearer at her funeral service at Washington's National Cathedral. After Rachel's death, Bob donated 135 of his original drawings from *The Edge of the Sea* to the Rachel Carson collection at Yale's Beinecke Library. Even his return address on the brown wrapping paper of the package, preserved in the Carson papers, displays a creative flair. The image depicts the drawn outline of an artist's palette with a few brushes tucked within the thumb-hole; he then printed his name and address within the border of the palette.

Hines's connection to Carson continued throughout the forthcoming decades. In 1980, Hines received an invitation to a luncheon at the White House when President Carter posthumously awarded the Presidential Medal of Freedom to Carson. (At that event, Hines's colleague Roger Tory Peterson also received the same award.) Bob referred to the White House invitation as "the highest of highlights of my life." Hines's last major commission was the illustrations for a fiftieth anniversary edition of *Under the Sea-wind*, Carson's first book, released in 1991. Bob fondly recalled his association with Rachel Carson: "I think Rachel was probably about the greatest lady I will ever know. She had friends worldwide, and they saluted her not just for her knowledge and ability, but also for her personality. She was really a great one."

Chapter 8

Wildlife on Postage Stamps

The genesis of a wildlife postage stamp began when Ed Kalmbach, designer of the 1941 Federal Duck Stamp, first proposed the notion to the US Postal Service in 1949. Postmaster General Jesse M. Donaldson already had declined a previous request for a stamp commemorating the centennial of the Interior Department. Donaldson relayed in a letter to Interior Secretary Krug: "Nothing would give me more pleasure than doing this for you, but there is not time enough to put out this issue. If there were sufficient time, I have my doubts about commemorating the anniversaries of the various departments of the government through the issuance of a commemorative stamp. We did not do it for the Post Office Department."

Kalmbach, then director of the Wildlife Research Laboratory in Denver, petitioned his Colorado senators Edwin Johnson and Eugene Millikin, encouraging them to support the issue of US postage stamps that would commemorate North American wildlife. Noting the enactment of the Duck Stamp Act of 1934 followed by the Pittman Robertson Act, which provides federal funding to states for wildlife restoration projects, Kalmbach stated, "[T]here is no question that the 15 years subsequent to 1934 have been the most dynamic in the field of wildlife conservation since the founding of the nation." In his letters, Kalmbach nominated "subjects for United States commemorative stamps honoring wildlife resources." He also included his rendition of different species in a trial design suggesting their possible depiction on a stamp. Postmaster General Donaldson remained unmoved. In a reply letter to Senator Millikin, he returned the senator's letter and Kalmbach's model drawings. Donaldson concluded his letter with the disclaimer, "For the present, we have on hand far more meritorious applications for commemorative issues than can possibly be given the desired attention. I appreciate the views submitted in this matter and wish to compliment Mr. Kalmbach upon the attractiveness of his wildlife designs."

Kalmbach refused to accept defeat. In a 1950 article for *Nature* magazine, he presented an overview of wildlife depicted on postage stamps from other countries around the globe. Interspersed throughout the text are additional samples of Kalmbach's designs for stamps featuring various species of American wildlife. In 1952, Sam Neel, a prominent Washington attorney and sportsman, approached Hines to purchase some original artwork for his personal collection. Neel expressed an interest in obtaining a print of Kalmbach's 1941 Duck Stamp design. In the spirit of networking, Hines provided Neel with Kalmbach's contact information. During a meeting in Denver between these two men, the conversation drifted to the notion of wildlife postage stamps. Enlightened, Neel returned to Washington and queried Hines why the Information Office of the Fish and Wildlife Service (FWS) never promoted a wildlife stamp series.

By 1953, Kalmbach wrote to Hines regarding the "road block" he encountered with the Post Office Department. Kalmbach alluded to his 1949 letter from Senator Millikin suggesting "that I may want to go into the matter again at a later date if there is 'any change in the Department's situation.' I can put only one interpretation on the latter expression; namely, when there is a change in administration, which has now occurred." Kalmbach concluded: "One last and very important point which I wish to make is that the designs which I have prepared should be construed only as a suggestion to visualize the idea. Certainly there are many more competent artists in the country (including yourself) who could do a very much better job."

Neel then conceived an approach where Hines would paint four species of trout—brown, brook, rainbow, and cutthroat—to be earmarked as gifts for President Eisenhower. Businessman Aksel Nielson, an advisor to the president who would accompany him on a Colorado fishing expedition, would be the intermediate. Nielsen agreed to present the paintings to Eisenhower during his forthcoming vacation in Denver. Meanwhile, Hines began working on the paintings as a personal project on his own time at home.

By the time of the presidential fishing trip in September 1955, Hines had completed the brook and brown trout paintings. Neel wrote to Nielsen about the proposed wildlife conservation stamps: "I still think this is an acceptable program for the Administration to sponsor. I don't see how it is subject to criticism from any source. On the contrary, why would it not be a remarkably apt vehicle to effectively meet some of the attacks that people . . . have been making on the Administration claiming that the Administration is not truly interested in conservation of natural resources?" Neel was referring to the recent criticism of a federal plan to construct a dam that would flood Echo Park, a remote corner of Dinosaur National Monument along the shared borders of Utah and Colorado.

Decades after a similar project inundated pristine Hetch Hetchy Valley within California's Yosemite National Park, a favorite location of John Muir, environmentalists rose in numbers to protest the desecration of such a scenic public land supposedly preserved for perpetuity. With such an outcry from the citizenry, government officials later cancelled their plan to construct the dam. Neel continued, "I would like to present the proposal to [President Eisenhower] along with two beautiful original watercolors of trout Bob Hines has made for him." Neel concluded: with "Please remember we don't represent anybody in this but ourselves. It still seems to me to be a 'natural' both for this Administration and the outdoors which you and I and the President all enjoy so much."

Mr. Nielsen presented the unframed artwork to the president and advocated the proposed commemorative wildlife stamps. Neel had drafted a proposal for the president that included: "Such a series would be tremendously popular and would be welcomed by all those thousands of individual citizens and groups throughout the country, who in recent years have become more and more vocal in promoting wildlife conservation. Since this proposal does not originate from any organized group and would not honor any special interest or individual, it would avoid the criticism that most proposed commemorative issues usually generate."

The gesture impressed President Eisenhower such that he dictated a letter to Postmaster General Arthur Summerfield: "The attached file, handed to me by a good friend of mine, has a very strong appeal for me. I should like very much to see designated and issued this year a series of stamps featuring the wildlife of the United States as one factor in conservation of natural resources."

Summerfield quickly replied: "The proposal appeals to me very much. I will, immediately upon my return to Washington, explore the idea of a series of 'Wildlife Stamps' with our people of the Philatelic Division."

Later that month, Aksel Nielsen reported back to Sam Neel: "I did give the President your pictures and he had them up at the ranch. I am sure he is looking forward to the other two pictures as well." Hines and his colleagues savored their triumph. Ed Kalmbach predicted that the Hines's trout paintings one day would occupy a prized spot on the wall of Eisenhower's home in Gettysburg, Pennsylvania. However, that vision never came to fruition. President Eisenhower sustained a major heart attack while on his western vacation. During the president's prolonged hospitalization, the two Hines trout paintings disappeared, presumably stolen from Lowry Air Force Base, Eisenhower's "Summer White House." Bob's superiors received instructions allowing him to repeat replacement paintings. Hines completed the brown trout, but the piece remained in his personal collection, never making it to the president.

The FWS remained in the communication loop regarding plans for the wildlife stamps largely because of Hines's employment in the organization. An undated and unsigned memo nominated four species of wildlife as possible subjects for the forthcoming stamps—pronghorn antelope, largemouth bass, wild turkey, and Canada goose. Excessive hunting had decimated the pronghorn antelope population to a few small herds with a total of around 17,000 animals. Contemporary game and land management increased the numbers such that five western states resumed open hunting seasons to control the number of antelopes. A native of the Southeast and Midwest, the largemouth bass became amenable to hatchery propagation, allowing it to be transplanted widely to nearly every continental state. After generations of over-hunting, the wild turkey responded favorably to stocking efforts throughout much of its former range. The Canada goose, the emblem of the Service's National Wildlife Refuge system, likewise expanded its range with transplantation, game management, and provision of adequate habitat.

Further discussion altered the list of proposed species. Members of the Service's Division of Information suggested substituting the king salmon for the largemouth bass, as the latter "was more representative of the broad responsibilities of the Federal Government, which involved the management of commercial fisheries." Hines reported that this was "an effort to select typically American species representing birds, mammals, and fish. Each of the selected species has been the subject of intense research and management by both Federal and State organizations, and each of the species has benefited from conservation practices." The whooping crane was perhaps most emblematic of modern wildlife conservation efforts. Once more geographically widespread, the numbers of whooping cranes plummeted in the nineteenth century because of unregulated hunting and habitat loss as a result of westward settlements. Perched on the brink of extinction from a critical low of fourteen birds in the early 1940s, the population increased to around thirty the following decade thanks to aggressive management techniques. Thus, the whooping crane surpassed the Canada goose as a candidate for depiction on the planned series of postage stamps.

As news of the forthcoming stamps reached the media, Thomas Kimball, director of Colorado's Department of Game and Fish, wrote directly to President Eisenhower requesting "that the initial release of the antelope stamp be in Denver. I think it would be equally fitting that the wild turkey stamp be released in the East where the colonists first encountered this great American game bird, and that the salmon stamp be released in the Pacific Northwest where this fish has always been present."

The Postal Service entrusted Hines with the designs for the first four wildlife stamps. He started with several preliminary drawings, while his colleagues at the Service selected the most representative one for each species. Hines then detailed each image employing a wash technique. For the penultimate step, the Bureau of Engraving applied the margins, lettering, and denomination to complete the prototype image prior to the final engraving. Bob shared his antelope rendition with colleagues Sam Neel and Aksel Nielsen. In a letter to Neel, Nielsen revealed, "I showed [the antelope drawing] to a fellow who probably knows more about what a picture of an antelope looks like than anyone else, and he says it's impossible for him to fault it."

The wild turkey stamp was the first release in the series. This event occurred on May 5, 1956, in Fond du Lac, Wisconsin, coinciding with the Silver Anniversary Convention of the Wisconsin Federation of Stamp Clubs. The *Fond du Lac Commonwealth Reporter* announced: "All attention of the stamp collecting world was centered on the post office Saturday when the US postal department issued the first of a series of three-cent wildlife stamps." Assistant Postmaster General Robert E. Fellers gave the principal address during the ceremony at the Crystal Ballroom of Hotel Retlaw. Discussing the species depicted on the forthcoming series of stamps, he emphasized, "We wanted to be absolutely certain that the final selections were the best examples of the important need for wildlife conservation as well as true representatives of American wildlife." Fellers discussed how the once common wild turkey had reached its population nadir, because of unregulated hunting, a trend that reversed with reintroduction and timely game management.

Fond du Lac Postmaster Louis J. Andrew hired "50 extra women employees" to accommodate stamp sales and first-day cancellations. The local post office received 1.5 million of the new stamps and coordinated some 200,000 post-marked cancellations. An estimated one thousand visitors attended the philatelic convention at the hotel. After the first-day sale in Fond du Lac, the remainder of the 120 million wild turkey stamps became available at the 39,000 post offices across the country.

The pronghorn antelope stamp was the next release, which occurred on June 22, 1956, in Gunnison, Colorado. The event was held in conjunction with the thirty-first annual convention of the Colorado Division of the Izaak Walton League of America. Contrasted with the brisk attendance at the Fond du Lac event, the outdoor ceremony in front of Webster Hall attracted a "discouragingly small crowd." Postmaster B. H. Snyder hired "30 women" to process the 200,000 stamps that had been purchased prior to the actual first-day sale. In a small, local post office that was ill equipped to handle such a disproportionately large volume of mail, the community banded together to process 461,000 first-day cancellations. Collectors requested single stamps up to a plate block of four stamps per envelope; air-mail letters required five stamps for adequate postage. As with the wild turkey design, the Postal Service requested an initial printing of 120 million of the antelope stamps.

Hines attended the Gunnison reception as a representative of the FWS. He traveled by air from Columbus to Denver, then by automobile to the ceremony in Gunnison. Hines recalled: "One of our agents drove, and he took me over and through some of the high passes. [W]e threw snowballs and drank ice water. [A]t Gunnison they put me in a rubber boat with the local game protector, and we went floating down the Gunnison River. It is clear and fast, and the rocks bulged the bottom of the boat. . . . [W]e caught a few trout, but not many. . . ."

Returning to Denver by a different route, "mule deer and marmots, and ravens and golden eagles showed themselves. A weekend in Denver . . . meant that I got in on two steak barbecues, wherein they bring in a steer for each guest, lop off the head and tail, and expect you to eat all the in-between. No foolin! [T]hose steaks were three inches deep and DEElichus." Hines then went to Salt Lake City where he toured Bear River National Wildlife Refuge both by land and by small plane. "Quite a place, even without the big flocks that come down in the fall." He departed by air for Jackson Hole "through the Teton Range. The best mountains this side of Alaska."

Spending five days in the National Elk Refuge, he collected some "bugs and butterflies" for his son Johnny who had developed a fascination for insects. "It tickles me when I come in with some species that he does not have, and even more so when he has trouble identifying them."

"Trumpeter swans and sand hill cranes, mule deer and elk, and lotsa trout. We drove to Yellowstone Lake for one day, and I got tired of catching cut-throat trout." He "got enough sketches to complete the painting for the President. (If only they would allow me enough time to complete those paintings.) A cinnamon bear chased me back into the car. [T]he photo I took of him shows that I moved fast—the image and background are both fuzzy, but you can see his lowered head and feet off the ground—all headed straight at the lens." Hines neglected to report an emergency that arose while fishing at Yellowstone Lake: His companions had to remove a fishing hook that had lodged in Bob's scalp while he was casting his fishing line.

The Salmon Industry of the Northwest and the Seattle Chamber of Commerce cosponsored the king salmon stamp release on November 9, 1956. Contrary to the activities surrounding the release of the first two stamps at their respective venues, which provided grist for the smaller local newspapers, there was little media coverage in the Seattle newspaper. Of the 120 million stamps printed, the Seattle post office expected to sell at least one million stamps over the weekend of its debut. One collector told a reporter, "This publicizes our salmon industry and Greater Seattle. [I]t is the first issue we have had from Seattle since 1949." Hines's name appears as illustrator on the programs from Fond du Lac and Gunnison, but his name is absent on the Seattle program. However, Tom Duncan recalls the enjoyment he had driving Hines around Seattle during the time of the king salmon stamp ceremony.

As 1956 approached its close, the FWS awarded $500 and a Certificate of Merit to Hines. The gesture recognizes Hines's "contribution to our conservation objectives by promoting successfully the current series of wildlife postage stamps as well as designing the first three stamps in the series." Service Director John Farley praised Hines for his "interest, initiative, and talent," adding, "this creative act is a valuable effort in the direction of publicizing wildlife conservation." Earlier Hines had shared the preliminary news with Rachel Carson: "MacBain [Bob's supervisor at the Service] has memoed the Interior Incentive Awards Committee [on] my behalf, presenting the history, method of creating, and achievements of these stamps. [A]nd maybe . . . they will pay some attention to the memo. Perhaps even pay some green stuff to me."

The first three wildlife stamps were printed using the intaglio method, featuring Hines's clean designs against a monochromatic hue. In 1957, the Bureau of Printing and Engraving purchased a Giori press, which produced multicolored stamps in a single pass. An American flag stamp featuring the national colors of red, white, and blue was the first stamp released using the new Giori press.

The Bureau had grand plans for a multicolored fourth Wildlife Conservation stamp. The whooping crane stamp depicts two white adult cranes against a blue background standing with two golden downy chicks on a green grassy base. Plans for the official release on November 22, 1957, included events at the National Postage Stamp Show in New York City and in Corpus Christi, Texas. The latter venue's significance lies in its proximity to the whooping cranes' wintering ground at Aransas National Wildlife Refuge on the Gulf coast of Texas. The New York show, held at the seventy-first Infantry

Regiment Armory at Park Avenue and 34th Street, employed "The Wildlife of America" as its overall theme. In an interoffice memo, Hines reported, "The theme of this huge show will be wildlife conservation. [T]he entire armory will be decorated on this theme, emphasizing the wild turkey, the antelope, and the salmon stamps of 1956, with special prominence given to the whooping crane of 1957. This show will be given complete international coverage by television, radio, newspapers, and magazines. Mr. Keller [the coordinator of the show] is interested in having Fish and Wildlife Service personnel take part in the ceremony, offering us one of the finest chances in recent years to present our program to the public."

Publicity prior to the New York event predicted over 70,000 expected visitors and over 100,000 first-day cancellations that would be posted. Those estimates were conservative—final accounting after the show revealed over 2 million stamps sold with over 284,000 covers posted. Hines was present at the Armory to autograph stamps and covers, signing them "Bob Hines, stamp artist."

Carl Reuth, editor of *Linn's Weekly Stamp News*, conducted his annual survey of philatelists for 1956. Respondents selected Hines's pronghorn antelope stamp as the best design for an American stamp that year; the wild turkey stamp was number three, while the king salmon stamp figured in at number eight. The following year's survey selected the whooping crane stamp as number two, trailing behind the American flag ("Long May It Wave"). Hines received even more prestige in the British 1959 Stamp Collector's Annual. L. E. Scott chose Hines's whooping crane design as one of the ten best stamps for the world in 1958. Scott declared that although the stamp had an official release late in 1957, that year's Annual had already gone to press. Thus, Scott took the liberty of including the whooping crane stamp in his 1958 tally.

Initial plans were to continue the wildlife conservation series for a number of years. In the aforementioned letter to Rachel Carson, Hines shared that the Postal Service "will consider one wildlife conservation stamp a year for the next ten years. . . . MacBain and his art staff [that is, Hines] are both delighted with the prospect, especially since the FWS has again been assigned as designer, final authority, chief contributor, etc of all such stamps. Even if the election this fall changes things, we feel that the chances are pretty good, for even Democrats couldn't ignore the flavor of some of the clippings we have about the reception given these stamps."

With a later Service memo, Hines detailed: "To continue this series I have asked for an appointment with Mr. Rohe Walter, Special Assistant to the Postmaster General, to outline a several years' program and to nominate species for future stamps. I expect to nominate the fur seal as the top nominee for 1958." Unfortunately, the series lost its momentum. Another set of four American wildlife conservation stamps would not appear until 1971, now with a denomination of eight cents. The following year, a subsequent set of four more stamps were released, the fur seal being one of the species depicted. Hines had no involvement in the design of these two series.

Bob became acquainted with the compulsive side of philatelists during the release of the wildlife conservation stamps. His wild turkey image depicts a solitary bird flying against a background of conifers. Hines had inquiries from stamp collectors inquiring as to the species of pine tree on his design. Bob was also nonplussed to learn that some philatelists counted the number of perforations around the margin of each stamp.

Social dynamics and burgeoning technologies continued to isolate Americans from their natural roots during the post–World War II years. The series of wildlife stamps, which had a total press run of nearly 5 million individual stamps, introduced the word *conservation* to the general public, a decade before the concept penetrated the national consciousness. Though an employee of the Service only eight years by the time the whooping crane stamp was released, Hines had several other opportunities ahead to educate the laity on natural history and wildlife conservation.

Chapter 9

The Eye of a Nation

As staff artist for the Fish and Wildlife Service (FWS), Hines welcomed the challenge of capturing his subjects in detail to the satisfaction of experts in various disciplines affiliated with the organization. At times, his confidence would ebb, cognizant of his lack of education beyond high school as he interacted with highly educated colleagues. Occasionally, Bob's immediate supervisors, biologists or wildlife management men by training, had little insight into the artistic process. These bureaucrats could not comprehend why Hines's wellspring of creativity would not obey the rigid time clock confines of a government office routine. Frequently, the boundary between work day and personal time blurred as Bob continued his work assignments at home while the muse of artistry remained with him.

Hines enjoyed interacting with young people, ever mindful of how the Boy Scouts rescued him from the void of grief after his beloved mother's untimely death as he crossed the threshold of adolescence.

Back in the days when he worked for the Ohio Division of Conservation and Natural Resources in Columbus, Bob developed a program of "chalk talks," which he typically gave when there was an event with a youthful audience. Accompanied with chalk and a large pad of paper elevated on an easel, he would draw an animal while he extemporaneously gave a short lesson on its physical features or habits, weaving a tale from his personal experiences in the out-of-doors. Hines saw no reason to discontinue this tradition after he transitioned to federal employment. During the 1959–60 season, the National Park Service sponsored a Nature Adventure Club, the activities of which attracted over six thousand visitors. For his contribution, Bob held two "Adventures with Wildlife" sessions in the Interior Building's spacious auditorium. In a letter of appreciation, the superintendent of the National Capital Parks reported: "Mr. Hines demonstrated considerable skill in holding the attention of the overflow audiences of young people, with his entertaining and informative chalk talk on wild animals he had known in the Washington area. His presentation, with its pleasing personal touch, was important in helping us give a well-rounded story of the wildlife of National Capitol Parks. We are grateful for the contribution of Mr. Hines' time and talent, and we feel that he admirably represented the Fish and Wildlife Service."

Robert Glotzhober, a naturalist with the National Wildlife Federation, recalled his encounter with Hines in a later decade:

> *For National Wildlife Week we always had a big public celebration, and one year Bob Hines came and presented a chalk talk on the lawn. Most of it was drawing in chalk by request of kids in the crowd—who were then awarded with the drawing to their great glee. At one point Bob started an un-requested drawing, not telling us what it would be at the start. Taking a block of black chalk, he started making large, sweeping black lines on the page. I don't think anyone could imagine what animal he was drawing. Then, quite suddenly, a white whooping crane popped off the page to the group's astonishment! It was quite a thrill and he impressed me not only with his art, but with his warm and friendly relationship with the audience.*

Hines received a surprise endorsement in 1960 that lifted his spirits. J. N. "Ding" Darling was the esteemed Pulitzer Prize—winning political cartoonist, former head of the Bureau of Biological Survey (a predecessor to the FWS), and designer of the very first Federal Duck Stamp. Darling complimented Hines's artistry, comparing his work to that of two other legendary wildlife artists:

I remembered, in the middle of the night, that I neglected to comment on the work of Bob Hines in my letter which was mailed yesterday. I have had it in mind for a long time to speak about the high quality of his wildlife illustrations. Over the years that I have been associated with wildlife conservation I have watched many wildlife artists come and go and I've been quite well acquainted with some of them. . . . Lynn Bogue Hunt was awfully good, and so were a lot of others, but I never saw anyone who could equal Bob Hines in the black-and-white delineation of fish and wild fowl, unless perhaps it would be Lee Jaques, and even Lee has to have color to make his pictures pop the way Bob Hines' does. Please extend to him my congratulations. Bob Hines is so very good that it seems to me a shame to load him up with a lot of routine duties which must certainly cut down on his time to make pictures. That fellow is 'way out front as a draftsman and he ought not to have anything else to do.'

By 1960, Hines's salary for the position of illustrator was $8,600 per year, slightly more than twice the amount of his starting salary when he joined the Service a dozen years prior. As this new decade dawned, the inauguration of youthful President John F. Kennedy ushered in an era of palpable energy and promise. Kennedy selected Arizona Congressman Stewart Udall as his Interior Secretary. Together, they embarked on an ambitious program of land acquisition for public use. Another emphasis of Udall's tenure was the education of the public regarding US natural heritage. Hines's talents were well suited for the number of high-profile publications that the Service would release in the near future.

As the decade of the 1950s waned, the country's midwest region sustained a serious drought such that 50–80 percent of the prairie potholes, the prime nesting habitat for waterfowl, were lost in the Dakotas and Canada. Speaking at the annual meeting of the Outdoor Writers Association of America in Hot Springs, Arkansas, in June 1959, Bureau of Sport Fisheries and Wildlife Director Dan Jantzen advised the writers to "have enough faith in the future of the sport to contribute three dollars for a duck stamp even though the hunting prospects look pretty grim." The reduced census of young birds translated into a decreased harvest; a poor hunting season might lead to fewer duck stamps sold, thereby reducing land and habitat acquisition through Duck Stamp revenue.

Later that summer, Director Jantzen ordered a reduction of duck kill by one third to one half in all flyways except the Pacific. By the winter census, even the numbers of ducks in the Pacific flyway showed an 18 percent decrease. A survey during the early winter months of 1960 revealed a decline in the duck population by 20 percent across the continent. Three species—the redhead, canvasback, and ruddy duck—were especially affected. An announcement that summer foretold a closed season for canvasbacks and redheads in all four flyways.

First year canvasbacks had a nearly 50 percent annual mortality from hunting, while an estimated 25 percent of all species shot were either lost or crippled. The Bureau of Sport Fisheries and Wildlife launched a campaign to educate hunters about the closed season on certain species and to reduce the frequency of inaccurate shots. "Radio spots for hunter education" hit the airwaves:

> *Wait and let 'em come in until the eyes of the duck are visible. Here is some advice from an old duck hunter—if you can't see their eyes the ducks are not within shooting distance. Wait. Shoot to kill, not to cripple. Stop long range shooting. It cripples more ducks than it kills. Let the birds come in close. Don't be too eager to shoot those ducks. Let 'em come in close. Then you can identify the birds that can be taken only in limited numbers. And you will kill clean or miss clean and won't waste birds by crippling them.*

The hunter education also continued in print. Hines composed a visual chart that depicted the field identification marks of the three species that had additional protection—canvasbacks, redheads, and ruddy ducks. Another Hines graphic reinforced the message of proper hunting skills: "Minute men and oldtime hunters had something in common. Neither fired 'til the eyes were visible! Let 'em come in close then you kill clean or you miss clean."

The precarious numbers of canvasbacks and redheads were an impetus for correct field identification techniques. A conservation theme for the forthcoming Duck Stamp contest specifically stated that competing artists demonstrate a retriever in action. A zeitgeist for this era is Maynard Reese's 1959 Federal Duck Stamp design depicting the Labrador retriever King Buck clenching a fallen mallard drake in his mouth. The image reinforced the role of hunting dogs in decreasing the number of waterfowl lost to improper gunshots. As the hunting season concluded in early 1960, the sale of Duck Stamps had declined some twenty-five percent from the previous year. In an effort to encourage the sale of Duck Stamps to non-hunters, Hines created a certificate to display that year's stamp. The item vouches "That the holder of this document did purchase the attached Migratory Waterfowl Hunting Stamp as a contribution to the essential management and protection of these birds, which constitute so vital a part of the American wildlife heritage." The Bureau of Sport Fisheries and Wildlife promoted a nationwide campaign for such a nontraditional approach. A news release states, "In recognition of this support for conservation, an attractive, special certificate signed by Secretary of the Interior Fred A. Seaton, suitable for framing, has been prepared and will be given to each purchaser of a duck stamp at this time." The Service mounted another media campaign with a prominent plea, "Don't Shoot Us!" to remind hunters that "redhead and canvasback ducks are fully protected by law in the 1960–61 season." The announcement continues, "We must get as many of them as possible back to the breeding grounds. That's why there's no open season on these birds this year." It concludes with an admonishment, "Don't pull that trigger too quickly. Dead birds don't nest." A poster with this information bears Hines's line drawings of the two species of ducks.

Bob had contemplated the concept of a concise primer of waterfowl identification, something that would easily fit into a hunter's pocket. Hines recalled from his childhood that other boys could identify different airplanes by their silhouettes: "[T]hey knew by looking for certain field marks. So I transferred that knowledge and that way of looking to ducks." His prototype version was a simple accordion pleated, black-and-white illustrated sheet titled "Know Your Ducks. Field Guide for Hunters." Hines depicted seventeen ducks in flight as well as their profiles while swimming. One side of the guide groups ducks that fly with a vertical takeoff, the other those that gain flight with a running takeoff. The brief text encourages hunters: "Identifying ducks increases the pleasure of hunting. Learn how to do this. Then you can also save ducks which are scarce and shoot only those which are plentiful."

Bob then created material for a more detailed booklet. He stated, "I sent the rough draft of the manuscript and the layout of the drawings to my agent in New York, Marie Rodell. She sent it to five different publishers, and they all said they didn't want it." Frustrated with the lack of interest for a commercial release, Hines relinquished his opportunity for personal gain and entered the final draft into the public domain. Fortunately, the use of color to demonstrate identification traits was a permissible use of budgetary funds according to the Government Printing Organization (GPO). However, the colors appear rather subdued in the first run of this publication.

A Bureau press release from 1963 begins:

> *The Department of the Interior today urged that every waterfowl hunter taking to the field this fall equip himself with a thorough knowledge of the ducks and geese he seeks. This year's waterfowl regulations again stress the need for hunters to recognize their quarry before they pull the trigger. Enforcement officers probably will take a dim view of excuses that a hunter shot the wrong duck by "mistake," the Department said. To assist hunters this year, the Department has published a handy 24 page color waterfowl identification guide,* Ducks at a Distance.

The booklet, with its purchase price of twenty-five cents, "was especially prepared to show waterfowl in their fall migration colors and to portray the birds from the same perspective that hunters see them in the wild." Within months of its release, *Ducks at a Distance* had "broken into the roster of the current 'best sellers' of Government publications."

A subsequent press release offers: "Each of the booklet's 88 color drawings was carefully composed by wildlife artist Bob Hines of the Fish and Wildlife Service to depict the birds in the colors and detail that would normally be seen by a birdwatcher or hunter at a distance. The booklet also contains a unique scaled comparison of the shapes and sizes of all the common varieties of ducks and geese."

According to Hines, *Ducks at a Distance* became "the first best seller that the Department of Interior ever published in the last 40 years. Before that there was one from the Bureau of Mines on safety."

With the placement of *Ducks at a Distance* in the public domain, the release appeared nationwide as a twin-page layout in the full-color comics section of several newspapers. Hines's superiors agreed to give him a $450 cash award for his time and effort that made *Ducks at a Distance* such a success. Because of the booklet, the Wildlife Society later presented Hines a Conservation Education Award at its annual banquet held at the Statler Hilton Hotel in Washington, DC.

An unexpected benefit from the preparation of *Ducks at a Distance* was the opportunity for Hines to work with Pete Anastasi, a relationship that evolved into a strong friendship.

Pete was born in Philadelphia, Pennsylvania, the son of immigrant Italian parents. In his youth, the Anastasi family moved to Syracuse, New York, where Pete spent his formative years. Coming of age during those Great Depression years, Pete began working for a produce company to support the family upon the death of his father. After a stint in the US Army that included a tour of North Africa, Pete returned to his former employer. Following his marriage to Betty, a young woman from Virginia, the newlyweds decided to move to her home state. Pete found employment as a salesman for Birmingham Dairy selling milk to various institutions in northern Virginia. Through the veteran's bureau, he learned of a job opportunity at the GPO. Despite a cut in pay from his work as a salesman, this new position offered training and the potential for advancement. After an unfulfilling two-year apprenticeship to become a pressman, Pete found his background in sales prepared him well to promote government publications for the general public.

One of Pete's first assignments was to advance the sales of *Ducks at a Distance*. He recalled, "Several million copies were sold, and I did all I could possibly [do] to promote this through news media, through radio, and personal presentations in different areas." Through Pete's efforts, the booklet later appeared in Spanish (*Los Patos a Distancia*) and French (*Guide d'identification des oiseaux aquatiques*) to aid hunters as well as nature aficionados in both hemispheres of the Americas. An outdoorsman at heart, Pete endeared himself to Hines when he revealed that he had shot the head off a turkey with a rifle bullet while the bird was in flight. Bob later immortalized that event on a retirement collage for Pete. Hines and Anastasi became fast friends who enjoyed each other's company with their outdoor adventures. Bob would remind his own children of the maxim "you cannot choose your family, but you can choose your friends." Pete recalled a time when he was pheasant hunting with Hines in northern Maryland. Bob shot at a bird, and in doing so cleanly severed the trunk of a respectable-sized sapling. The crown of the tree momentarily remained suspended in the air above the stump before it crashed onto the ground. After a preternatural interval of quiet, a wide-eyed Hines turned to his hunting companion and dryly replied, "Now you know what a shot will do to you."

Bob desperately needed the mooring of a good friendship. Living alone, separated from his family, led to dark moods of melancholy that casual affairs and loveless relationships only aggravated. The physical as well as emotional separation between Bob and his wife Edna affected all members of the Hines family. Edna shouldered the responsibility of child rearing and discipline. Though legally estranged, she faced the stigma of being an essentially single mother during an era when divorce was not socially acceptable. At a time when few women worked outside their homes, Edna became the aquatic director for the YWCA in Columbus, Ohio. She traveled widely as coach for the Coralinas, the local synchronized swimming team.

One winter, Edna went to Texas for a swim meet while Bob remained in the Washington area. Son John, a budding entomologist, went to a local spot in Ohio with two friends to collect snow fleas. John slipped off a rocky escarpment and fell head first into an ice-covered pond. When he regained his senses, he found himself trapped underwater breathing in sand and silt. One of his companions ran a considerable distance around the shore of the pond until he found John's legs within the broken ice. While that friend dragged John out of the frigid water, the other one departed to summon an ambulance. A local hospital evaluated John then transferred him to the Ohio State University Hospital, all this with both of his parents away in different states. Fortunately, the hypothermia that John sustained protected his brain from deterioration; he recovered fully from his accident. When Bob learned that John's condition was stable, he did not return to Ohio. Rather he completed a painting for each of his son's rescuers as a gesture of appreciation for their heroic efforts. One young man, who had an interest in wildlife biology, received a painting of a wolverine; the other friend received a painting of a sea horse because of his interest in marine biology.

Notwithstanding Edna's active lifestyle and level of physical fitness, her girlhood adversary of rheumatic fever reemerged in a sinister manner. As Edna's mitral valve began to narrow, she developed signs of congestive heart failure. Heart valve replacement was in its infancy at this time. Edna's family inquired about the possibility of having her travel to see Dr. Michael DeBakey, the renowned heart surgeon in Houston, Texas. However, as Edna's heart started to beat irregularly, a shower of blood clots led to a stroke, disqualifying her as a candidate for surgery. Succumbing to her rheumatic heart disease, Edna Hines died at fifty-four years of age in December 1965.

Bob made the sad trip back to Columbus to help plan the funeral for the mother of his children. Edna's obituary in the Fremont newspaper states "surviving are her husband, also a Fremont native and a widely known artist" along with her two children. The product of a generation that did not encourage the public display of a man's emotion, Bob reprimanded his son John when he wept at his mother's funeral. As a testament to the discord between Bob Hines and his mother-in-law, Vera Beatty refused to include Edna's surname by marriage on the family's pink granite tombstone in Fremont's Oakwood Cemetery.

Less than eight months after Edna Hines's death, Bob shocked his children with the news that he had married Nancy Hays Miller. His pronouncement, "You now have a new mother," reflected insensitivity to his children's grief over the recent loss of their own mother.

Nancy was born in central Pennsylvania in 1925. After her marriage failed in 1949, she left her young son with her parents in Pennsylvania then moved to the Washington, DC, area to accept a secretarial job with the Bureau of Mines in the Interior Department. After a short stint in that position, Nancy transferred to the FWS, Division of Information, where she worked for Rex Schmidt, the section chief and a colleague of Bob Hines. It was at that time that she first became acquainted with Hines. By 1952, Nancy remarried and assumed the surname of Trahan. The following year, she transferred out of the Interior Department to the National Zoological Park. She worked there only about eight months until she resigned according to her personnel folder "because of ill health upon the advice of my physician." Nancy had inherited a propensity for alcoholism from her father. The dissolution of her second marriage along with her abuse of alcohol are the most plausible reasons for her health issue at that time.

One year later in the spring of 1955, Nancy reapplied for a secretarial appointment in the National Zoo. She subsequently requested a name change back to Nancy H. Miller. A photograph of her appears in a *National Geographic* magazine article on zoo animals. In the image, she bottle feeds Frances and Elizabeth, twin bear cubs, both a second-generation hybrid cross between polar and brown bears. Nancy presents a striking image with her wavy brunette hair in a short cut, her red lipstick and fingernails contrasting with a yellow turtleneck shirt. Nancy worked for the National Zoo for a full decade until she resigned in January 1966, her personnel file revealing that she needed to return to Pennsylvania to take care of her ill mother, Daisy Hays. Bob Hines had a fondness for Daisy. Still receptive to a maternal influence during his adult years, Hines carried her name and address among his contact information during his Alaskan assignment in the autumn of 1954.

Edward Plunkett, a Methodist minister, married Bob and Nancy in a private ceremony on July 22, 1966, in northern Virginia. A handful of friends from the Service, including Pete and Betty Anastasi, as well as some of Nancy's coworkers from the National Zoo attended a small reception at one of the local hotels. In a Christmas card to a friend, Bob wrote: "The double signature on this card is because I have finally remarried—the 1st wife died just before Xmas last year, and I never did get to send any greetings. Nancy is a former Fish & Wildlife lady, and we are more than happy." Despite the marriage's propitious start, there was turbulence to follow. Nancy became a member of Alcoholics Anonymous; Bob supported her attempts to regain her sobriety whenever her drinking relapsed.

Prior to the construction of the Interior Building in 1935, Secretary Harold Ickes approved the addition of two eighth-floor aeries that were subsequently dubbed penthouses. The south penthouse became an employee lounge area. The north penthouse was earmarked into a studio for government radio broadcasts that advanced the tenets of the New Deal. During the Truman administration, the "Voice of America" broadcasts originated from the same locus. After television superseded radio as the principal medium reaching most American homes, the north penthouse gradually lost its historical use and became office space for the National Park Service and the FWS.

In the 1960s, Bob Hines moved into his new office in the north penthouse, its walls still lined with perforated acoustic tiles. Bob's solitary office window faced eastward to a horizontal vista of seemingly endless gravel rooftops. To the north, one could appreciate the slightly hipped roof of the White House. Hines recalled the day he watched seven bald eagles circle over the presidential residence. Bob elaborated, "all they were doing was circling, not interfering one with the other. It looked more like a kettle of buzzards up there. Had I not seen the white on the tails and heads of some of them, I might have been fooled, too." He also observed some forty species of birds that landed on the roof of the Interior Building as well as another thirty species that flew past his window. Bob revealed once that he had a gray fox cub up in his penthouse office. When Hines went downstairs for coffee, he would house the fox in a filing cabinet.

Bob still did relish the opportunity to travel outside of Washington. In 1963, he shared, "Your letter . . . was forwarded to me here at the Seney National Wildlife Refuge, where I have been working temporarily. Actually, I am having a ball, being surrounded by thousands of wild ducks and geese, deer, otters, grouse, and flying squirrels, and catching great northern pike. Since this is the first official field trip I have made for the Fish and Wildlife Service in seven years, you can understand that I am appreciating this Upper Peninsula, Michigan, woodland setting."

Later the regional director of the Bureau of Sport Fisheries and Wildlife in Minnesota expressed his appreciation for Hines's visit: "Mr. Hines provided valuable assistance and counsel in the preliminary planning of a large group of interpretive exhibits for the new visitor center now under construction at Seney. I might add that Mr. Hines worked diligently at Seney, despite the fact that he had not recovered from a bout with a virus infection and was also in considerable discomfort from a hip injury."

The penthouse, that nondescript room with its smoke-filled interior, roughly 9'×11', became a crucible for Hines's artistic output for the remainder of his time with the Service. A journalist described Bob's studio: "The office is what you might expect. Sketches are everywhere. On the drawing board are several crumpled paper towels requisitioned from the men's room. According to the artist, they make some of the best daubing sheets for removing excess paint or pointing up a brush. An ancient looking cart of coasters holds a ceramic paint dish, various tubes of paint and brushes. On the top sketch sheet, several new ducks float by."

Bob completed the numerous pencil drawings that illustrate chapter headings for *Waterfowl Tomorrow*, a compendium of waterfowl biology. Ambassadors Antonio Carrillo Flores of Mexico and Charles S. A. Ritchie of Canada joined Secretary Udall in a ceremony at the Interior Building upon the book's release in 1964. Udall acknowledged *Waterfowl Tomorrow* as a "milestone in international cooperation for the management and preservation of a great heritage—a heritage which nature destined the nations of our continent to share." He added, "Now, the best of our knowledge about migratory waterfowl, from all three of our nations, has been combined in a truly significant conservation work."

As the environmental movement began to crystallize, Secretary Udall declared in the book's foreword: "We and our children will be the losers if we do not care enough to save from exploitation some hills and dunes and swamps and woods and lakes where we can renew our ties to Nature and where God's other creatures can live and move and have their being. Let us not delude ourselves, or be content with sentimentality or mere words. The time has come when men must choose what kind of permanent relationship they want to have with their land and her creatures." He concluded, "It is for us to give conservation a new focus, a specific application not only to the broad fields of lands, forests, and water but also to the creatures that inhabit them." The book's overall thesis might have attracted a limited readership, but through the intervention of Pete Anastasi, *Waterfowl Tomorrow* received national media coverage.

As Hines's reputation continued to develop, he received an invitation to appear as a guest on the national television show "To Tell the Truth" in February, 1965. Though flanked by two male impostors, Bob's mastery of knowledge made him so transparent that the celebrity panelists had little trouble in guessing his true identity. An anonymous cartoon in Hines's files depicts the rear silhouettes of three men dressed in suits facing a studio audience. In the first pane, the "To Tell the Truth" host asks the men, "Will the real Bob Hines please give us a bird imitation?" In the second pane, as the men depart the stage, there is jubilation from the audience and consternation from the host as a gleaming speckled egg lies on the floor.

Birds in Our Lives, a high-profile 1966 release from the Bureau of Sport Fisheries and Wildlife, enlightens the general public on the wide spectrum in which birds affect society. As the editors state in their preface, "we believe the best way to achieve public support for sensitive management and conservation of birds is through a widening of public understanding of birds." Richly illustrated with many photographs, the hefty tome also includes a generous selection of Hines's original artwork created expressly for this book. His style ranges from loose abstractions that separate the book's nine sections to more detailed drawings that open each of the fifty-four chapters. The latter artwork occupies from one half to an entire substantially sized page. For the chapter that begins with the evolution of birds, staff members of the Smithsonian Institution gave Bob access to the casting of a fossilized Archaeopteryx skeleton from Bavaria. These colleagues also provided fossils of a tree trunk and leaves representative of the same geological period so that Hines could recreate an appropriate background for this prehistoric rendering. The chapter of "Tales Once Told" begins with a full-page, detailed black-and-white pencil drawing of a somber plumaged whippoorwill at rest on a leafy forest floor, a lady's slipper orchid blooming in the background. This composition depicts the Native American legend that the "moccasin flower" was the shoe of the whippoorwill, a nocturnal bird of mystery and superstition. For "Birds on Stamps," Hines recreated his design of the wild turkey from the 1956 Wildlife Conservation stamp along with a reproduction of the stamp itself.

In a press release from the Bureau of Sport Fisheries and Wildlife, Interior Secretary Udall commented, "*Birds in Our Lives* has a noble purpose and concept: To tell, in a simple, objective, and comprehensive way, about the uses, problems, needs, and present status of birds in the United States, so that Americans in all walks of life will be informed about them." The release mentions a price of nine dollars for the hardback volume.

In an incisive review in *Bird-Banding*, Elizabeth Austin gives an unflinchingly frank appraisal of the book with only a nominal mention of its artist, Bob Hines. "Two lines of an old rhyme about the sovereigns of England are applicable with changed tenses to the 61 authors of this book: 'Some are good and some are bad, but most of them are also in-betweens.' Most of the articles . . . are also in-betweens, neither very good or very bad." She continues, "The editor of this massive undertaking . . . should be congratulated on combining in any order at all such a heterogeneous collection of authors and subjects. The book is designed to inform readers to the influence of birds on their lives. This it will do very well, and it will not often misinform them. It will also show them where and how taxpayers' money is spent by the Bureau of Sport Fisheries and Wildlife and various other federal agencies." After a concise discussion of the book's shortcomings, Austin concludes, "All in all *Birds in Our Lives* is a very fine book, well illustrated and one of the best book buys of the decade."

When Arco Publishing Company released an abridged version of *Birds in Our Lives* in 1970, Austin was less complementary: "This is a reprint of parts of the excellent Fish and Wildlife Service publication of 1966. To reduce the size of the volume by 114 pages Arco has left out the most pertinent and timely essay in the original government printing . . . as well as fourteen other fine chapters. They have also carefully reprinted every error in the remainder—typographical and factual. Putting out an abridged version without marking it as such is misleading the public. Arco is asking just as much for their hardbound, chopped-up version as the federal government did for its complete publication. Although the paperback edition sells for one-third less, it is still no bargain. I suggest that anyone interested in owning *Birds in Our Lives* read my review in *Bird-Banding* and order an unmutilated version from the Superintendent of Documents, Washington, DC."

Perhaps the most impressive aspect of *Birds in Our Lives* is a full-color, full-page image of Hines's bald eagle rendering, which serves as the frontispiece of the government edition of the book. For many years, the original oil painting occupied a prominent location at the end of a corridor leading to the office of the director of the FWS in the Interior Building. In 1966, the Government Printing Office released a version of Hines's eagle reproduced as a collector's art print available from the GPO at a price of fifty cents.

With the environmental movement gaining momentum, Secretary Udall wrote: "Because the bald eagle is becoming increasingly rare, this illustration will have to replace the living bird for most citizens. The reasons for the eagle's decline are many, but they are apparently linked with a loss of habitat and possibly water pollution and pesticides. The Department of the Interior has established nesting places on its own wildlife areas to perpetuate the species, but they are fiercely independent and leave the sanctuaries. They thus become vulnerable to the hazards of environmental changes."

A press release describes the print as depicting "an adult eagle perched on a dead tree and silhouetted against an overcast sky above a rolling countryside. The eagle's wings are spread and its beak is open in a defiant scream."

Service photographer Luther Goldman captured the image of a beaming Secretary Udall holding the first bald eagle print as artist Bob Hines signs it. By the autumn of 1966, a newsletter for the Interior Department Recreation Association mentions that at that time over two hundred copies of the eagle print had been sold. The print experienced a revival a decade later. Christened "The Symbol of Our Nation," the timing of its release corresponded to the wave of patriotism during the nation's bicentennial year. With its price up to $1.85 a copy, the print sold well over one hundred thousand copies. Hines would sign copies of the eagle print as a gift to special visitors to the Interior Department. After a signed copy found its way to the Philadelphia Eagles, Hines and Pete Anastasi along with their wives enjoyed the comforts of a box seat one evening at an Eagles home game compliments of the team. During the half-time show of that particular game between the Eagles and the Dallas Cowboys, Bob's observant eye spied a peregrine falcon pursuing pigeons above the stadium. Hines recalled, "Nobody else was looking at it. [The falcon] was flying around in a circle, and nobody was looking. I looked [around] to see, and they were not watching it. There's life and death going right above their heads, and they never saw it. To me it's amazing!"

Joseph Linduska, associate director for the Bureau of Sport Fisheries and Wildlife, nominated Bob for an American Motor Conservation Award. Linduska elaborated, "Hines must be seen in light of his individual works, for each one is special. Cataloging, while helpful, does not really get at the rare ability we believe he possesses—the ability to put life into the illustrations of wild animals. . . . We believe his illustrations of wildlife are vibrant and real. . . . The ability to catch wildlife in the act of being alive—to stop action that precise moment which tells an entire story—this ability is part of the special quality Bob Hines puts into each painting. This life quality, a result of careful study and practice, is largely responsible for his appeal as an artist of wild things."

Hines had an affection for Okeefenokee National Wildlife Refuge, which straddles the state lines of Georgia and Florida. Earlier in his career at the Service, he had an opportunity to travel the refuge with Jewett Hall, a former trapper turned Service employee. Hall, born and reared in and around Okeefenokee, had knowledge and insight into the behaviors of the resident wildlife that any outdoors person would envy. Hall escorted Hines in a pirogue, which, Bob explained, is "one of those narrow, skinny boats. It's so narrow that if you get more air in one lung than in the other you're going to tip over." Hall showed how he could track a swimming otter. "He said, 'Look, he's been there. Watch, he's coming up right over here,' and he did. I would not have believed it. How this man can translate an otter's mind is something beyond my understanding." Bob sat in the bow of the pirogue while Jewett poled the boat from the stern. The shape of the pirogue did not allow it to negotiate sharp turns. As Hall propelled the boat, the momentum lifted Hines up into the bushes. "Now the bushes are all right, except that all of them had spider webs. I mean [with] big spiders. I'd be falling over backwards [while Jewett would] be back there cackling like mad."

One night, Hall took Hines out into the swamp to observe alligators. Jewett demonstrated how to view the reflection of an alligator's eyes in the dark, which must be done in parallax with the creature. The trees were punctuated with the reflection of spiders' eyes. Hines continued, "[Hall] said, 'There's a big gator there.' I said, 'I don't see it.' He [replied], 'Well he's right there,' and he gave a shove [of the boat.] The gator's head came up this side and the tail [went] up on [the other] side. I was right in the middle [in the] complete darkness. I got sopping wet and I hollered like a banshee. I tell you, if you were still down there you will find my hollering echoing around somewhere. I was scared, and I'll admit it."

The powers that be at the Bureau of Sport Fisheries and Wildlife approved a request for Hines to paint a mural for the visitor's center at Okeefenokee National Wildlife Refuge. He was eager to return to the area where he had such memorable experiences with Jewett Hall. Hines told a local reporter, "I love the place. It's a beautiful flower garden." This assignment was Hines's first large mural for the government in a dozen years. In 1968, Bob spent a month in the oppressive heat and humidity of the Georgia summer to complete the piece. Don Pfitzer, a Bureau colleague from the Atlanta Regional Office, visited Hines at the refuge. Don remembered the audible drone of squadrons of mosquitoes that the screens excluded. He photographed Bob, clad in a short-sleeved shirt and shorts, sometimes shirtless, composing his image of the waterscape. Hines chose to capture Chesser Island, a "prairie" on the eastern border of the refuge. The mural with its 8'×9' dimensions teems with wildlife, depicting a pair of ivory-billed woodpeckers along with bald eagle, osprey, swallow-tailed kite, pileated woodpecker, wood duck, great blue heron, black bear, and prothonotary warbler. One of Pfitzer's photographs documents that Hines also included a small flock of the now extinct Carolina parakeet in the lower right corner of the mural. Inexplicably, Hines painted over these particular birds, deleting them in the final version of the mural.

Pete Anastasi likewise visited Hines while he was on assignment at the Okeefenokee refuge. For a diversion from painting, Bob would cast his fishing line in a nearby pool. Once he called out, "Pete, I caught a big one!" Hines's excitement was short-lived when he learned that he had hooked one of the resident alligators. Bob severed his fishing line rather than risk a closer encounter with the reptile. Before Hines left the area, a concessionaire at the Suwannee Canal treated him to a different reptilian experience: a rattlesnake steak supper.

To acknowledge the centennial of fisheries conservation in the United States, the Bureau of Sport Fisheries and Wildlife released *Sport Fishing USA* in 1971. In preparation for this book, Hines's superiors approved the installation of a large aquarium, about five feet long and eighteen inches square on each end, in Bob's office. Members of the National Aquarium supplied the native fish—rock and small-mouth bass, bluegills, eels, white and yellow perch, as well as crayfish and an alligator snapping turtle. The antics of these piscine office mates inspired Hines to create the illustrations for *Sport Fishing USA*. He recalled, "Now a lot of people would say drawing a fish is easy. Well, it is if you know what you're drawing. From my way of looking at it, a fish has its own set of muscles and its own way of using them. They use their fins differently each time they want to do something, aggressive or recessive or flying or whatever. You have to show these things if you want to do a good job."

Frequently, there was friction between Bob and his supervisor who thought that Hines was wasting time by just sitting idle and watching the aquarium. Bob developed an unlikely ally when Secretary Udall's private secretary, Mrs. Fine, happened upon the penthouse office and spied the fishes. Intrigued by the aquarium's occupants, Mrs. Fine asked Hines to call her whenever he fed the fish. With that endorsement, even Hines's boss retreated in his criticism. Bob recalled that he spent seventy-nine cents a pound for medium shrimp at the local Giant supermarket. After freezing them in smaller bundles, Hines would chop the shrimp before he fed them to the fish and turtles three times a week. At feeding time, Bob reported, "it was a wild fight. The biggest fish got the shrimp pieces first. The smaller ones took what was left, and the turtles had to make do." One bold bass would pluck shards of food from the jaws of the snapping turtle. One day the bass took the entire turtle's head in its mouth and "slammed" the turtle around "like he was smoking a cigar."

By this time, modern printing techniques allowed more affordable color reproduction. This splashy volume includes an abundance of color photographs along with twenty-two full-color plates of various fish species that Hines painted in his penthouse office. The illustrations are remarkable in that they convey the habits as well as the habitats of their respective subjects. Even the covers of the book bear a split image color scene: the front depicts the energy of a leaping bass, mouth agape and gills splayed open as it loses an airborne lure; a pair of red-winged blackbirds along with two painted turtles at rest on a rock provide a more serene image on the back cover. Unlike the scholarly tone of the book's predecessors, *Sport Fishing USA* has an informal style that relates easily to the interests of the casual angler. A reviewer noted, "One doesn't rush through '*Sport Fishing U.S.A.*,' [rather] he glances at it, scans a page or two, then finds himself drawn into the words themselves as if pulled by a magnet." The writer then commented on Hines's "accuracy and meticulous detail."

Pete Anastasi endeavored to promote the new book with the local media. As a publicity stunt during a Washington Nationals baseball game, he had someone in the bleachers lower a copy of *Sport Fishing USA* on a fishing line down to the coach in the dugout. Hines received a letter from the assistant Secretary of Defense who commented on a display of *Sport Fishing USA* in the Pentagon's GPO bookstore: "There has been a tremendous interest shown here by all who have seen the display, and I am told that sales are doing extremely well. There is no question in my mind but that your exceptionally fine paintings which appear throughout the book are major contributors to its popularity."

As Hines's reputation as a wildlife artist widened, he continued to attract positive attention to the Department of the Interior. During the autumn of 1971, Interior Secretary Rogers C. B. Morton presented Hines the Distinguished Service Award. The citation reads as follows:

> *Robert W. Hines. In recognition of his outstanding contributions as a wildlife artist with the Bureau of Sport Fisheries and Wildlife. Robert Hines came to Washington twenty-two years ago and began work as an artist with the Fish and Wildlife Service. With several years['] experience, but with little formal training, he embarked on a career that has taken him over the country, sketching and painting wildlife. Mr. Hines understood that he had joined a highly scientific organization requiring great technical accuracy in its work, but also knew that his paintings would be seen not only by wildlife specialists but by many others—young children, businessmen, housewives, truck drivers, bankers, laborers—people who simply know that they enjoy wildlife and somehow realize it has an essential place in the natural world. Besides being technically accurate, his paintings would have to be infused with a quality of life. Through study and critical self-evaluation, he developed a characteristic style. His paintings became known for their accuracy and correctness. They also became known as works of art. Mr. Hines possesses a remarkable visual perception. He has used this rare gift to get down on canvas what many people see but do not realize they have seen until it is pointed out to them. He paints wildlife in the act of being alive. He has brought honor to his Bureau and Department. For his long service, for his continuing efforts to learn new things about his work, for his personal commitment that he shall never stop growing in his job, Mr. Hines is granted*

> *the highest honor of the Department of the Interior, the Distinguished Service Award.*

As Hines walked up to the stage to receive the award from Secretary Morton, he was so energized by the moment that Hines almost walked over the front of the stage rather than descend the opposite stairs. Morton shouted to Hines, "Hey, go over!" Bob recalled, "He saved my neck."

John Gottschalk, past director of the Bureau of Sport Fisheries and Wildlife, respected Hines and wished to promote his artistry. Gottschalk was instrumental in having the beautifully executed fish paintings from *Sport Fishing USA* reproduced into a set of ten collector's art prints titled "Wildlife Portraits No. 2." (Set No. 1 consists of photographs of endangered species.) Thus Hines's artwork gained further exposure to the general public. Undersecretary of the Interior and Mrs. William T. Pecora hosted a reception to meet the artist at the opening of "Game Fishes of America," an exhibit of paintings by Bob Hines at Washington's Adam's Rib Gallery in 1972.

In February 1972, Representative Delbert L. Latta of Ohio, Hines's home state, honored him by reading into the Congressional Record:

> *Mr. Speaker, we all appreciate rare and exceptional talent, particularly when it is used and made available for the benefit and enjoyment of all mankind. I am proud to call to the attention of my colleagues the artistic talents and endeavors of a very unusual man. I refer to Bob Hines, a longtime artist for the U.S. Department of the Interior.*
>
> *The Department of the Interior's Fish and Wildlife Service has just published "Wildlife Portrait Series No. 2" in its series of illustrations of America's fish and wildlife, part of a continuous program to help the public understand the need to preserve our environment. Set No. 2 contains reproductions of original paintings of fish by Bob Hines. . . .*
>
> *The Department of the Interior can be proud to have Mr. Hines on its staff, for his service to his fellow Americans is priceless. Each drawing is a reminder that unless we all help clean up America, future generations will see wildlife only through the eyes and drawings of an artist. . . .*

In 1913, the former Bureau of Biological Survey printed a booklet titled "Fifty Birds of Farm and Orchard" with color illustrations by the esteemed artist Louis Agassiz Fuertes. Decades later, the Bureau of Sport Fisheries and Wildlife put a new spin on that outdated publication with *Fifty Birds of Town and City*, released in 1975. A press release suggests that the book "is geared to the city dweller who knows little or nothing about birds . . . call it the 'non-birdwatcher's handbook' and you're on target." Discussing the changes from the book's predecessor the release continues, "The most obvious is that farms and orchards have been replaced by towns and cities. This has had a profound effect on the habits of many common birds—and of many people who have 'migrated' from farm to city." Moreover, the original Fuertes illustrations had faded with age such that reproduction would be less than optimal. The release continues rather floridly, "the paintings were redone by Bob Hines, Fish and Wildlife Service artist, who picked up that fallen Fuertes brush."

Hines and Anastasi were coauthors of this particular volume. Working together on other projects for a decade, Pete became aware of Bob's casual disregard for deadlines. Pete would fib by advancing the due date for Bob's artwork by a month, knowing that Hines would need extra time to complete his assignment before the material went to the printers. Anastasi promoted *Fifty Birds* with the media whenever possible.

Don Pfitzer recalled that Hines made an appearance at one of the Atlanta television stations. The set manager rushed up to Don and asked him in pressured speech, "Is something wrong with Mr. Hines? He's lying on the sofa!" Don casually replied, "Oh, he's just sleeping." On cue, Bob arose from his power nap and, without missing a beat, proceeded with his televised interview. After a visit to the Pfitzers' home in Atlanta that included some time watching birds at their backyard bird feeder, Hines sent his hosts a gift in appreciation of their hospitality, an original watercolor painting of brown headed nuthatches.

A selection of Hines's bird paintings became the basis for "Wildlife Portraits No. 4," another set of collector's prints. Bob supplemented this series with some quintessential western birds including the Steller's jay and acorn woodpecker. It was a common occurrence for Service employees to talk about birds in school rooms then donate a set of the Hines prints for their young audience to learn more about the resident birds of America.

In 1975, the Hines family experienced another milestone with the death of its patriarch George Hines. Bob maintained affection for his father, usually sending him an inscribed copy of the latest book that contained Bob's illustrations. The closeness between father and son is implicit in Bob's inscriptions. George's copy of *Birds in Our Lives* bears the handwritten message, "To my Father—to bring him pleasure and happiness, as he has to me." The copy of *Lost Wild America* states, "To My Dad ~ who has been inspiration, help, and ardent rooter ~ Bob Hines."

George Hines continued to work as a production manager at the Herbrand Company in Fremont, retiring around age seventy-five. After a change in corporate ownership, Hines learned that he had lost his retirement benefits. When George was eighty-six years old, his sons arranged to have him move from Fremont to an apartment in northern Virginia. George sent one of Bob's self-designed Christmas cards to a relative. With a measure of parental pride, George wrote in a shaky cursive, "This is one of Bob's inclusive [sic] painting[s]. Copies cannot be bought," adding, "Bob and Nancy live about one block from here." Another undated card with Bob's handwriting simply states, "Dad's 91, wheel-chaired, well nursed, fed, bathed and in good hands." George Hines maintained a cantankerous sense of humor, often pinching the nurses who attended to him. As George's health continued to decline, he transferred to a nursing home in Orange, Virginia, where he died of pneumonia one day after his ninety-fourth birthday. Rather than having George interred next to his beloved wife in Columbus, Ohio, his sons opted to return him closer to his boyhood home by scattering his cremains over Sandusky Bay.

The Abercrombie & Fitch Company (A&FC) acquired a reputation as a high-end supplier for sporting excursions, outfitting Theodore Roosevelt's African safaris. A&FC developed an art competition for a National Fish Stamp, closely patterned after the Federal Duck Stamp contest. A company catalog explains, "Identical in theme to the Federal Duck Stamp, which has been a collector's item for years, the National Fish Stamp was created to afford everyone the opportunity to contribute to the conservation of our country's sport fish and the waters they live in." Don Crowley's design of a brook trout plunging into flowing water appears on the first edition print and stamp. A Fish Stamp Kit consists of a color lithograph print along with one hundred printed stamps and one hundred "first day cover[s]" retailing for $100.

The catalog states that 25 percent of the proceeds would go to Trout Unlimited, the National Salmon Foundation, and the National Recreation and Park Association. This private contest piqued Hines's interest. He submitted an entry to the National Fish Stamp selection that depicts a leaping Atlantic salmon, the features of his rendering being a curious hybrid of a salmon and a muskellunge. The judges for the A&FC program selected Hines's design to appear on the following year's print and stamps. Bob received a cash prize of $1,000 along with an all-expenses-paid trip to the A&FC headquarters in New York City. Unfortunately, the company struggled to reflect its relevance in a modern society, closing its doors shortly after the release of Hines's stamp. A number of the prints found their way as complimentary gifts to raffles with a conservation theme.

Nancy H. Hines, Bob's second wife, inculcated a sense of financial responsibility into her artistic husband with his hedonistic pursuits. After a decade together of living in rental apartments, the married couple purchased a house. Following the death of Edna Hines, Bob sold the family home in Columbus, distributing the profits between himself and his two children. Bob's share of the proceeds went toward a small Cape Cod house on Key Boulevard in Arlington, Virginia. The finished second-floor level consisted of two rooms overlooking the street on the front of the house through dormer windows. Bob appropriated one of these spaces as his studio. In a Christmas card, Hines shared with a friend, "Our greatest pleasure was taking care of our house and yard—after 25 years in apartments, this is freedom. Had a great garden and have built an artificial bog. . . . [N]ext year we'll have yellow lady slippers and showy lady slippers blooming in it—and pink lady slippers right along side. Ferns and pitcher plants and marsh marigolds and all such."

After the inauguration of Jimmy Carter, the new president selected Idaho Governor Cecil Andrus as his Interior Secretary. Upon Hines's introduction to the newly arrived Secretary, Bob asked Andrus what he missed most about his home state. Andrus replied that he missed the fall elk hunting, which was a shared family event. Weeks later, Hines returned to the Secretary's office bearing a gift for Andrus—an oil painting of elk. Andrus remained amazed at Hines's ability to summon faithfully from memory the details of a bull elk with three cows against a backdrop of golden aspens that captures the splendor of autumn in the high Rockies.

Biologist Frederick Lincoln was the author of *Migration of Birds*, first published in 1935. A subsequent revision of the pamphlet appeared as a modest 1950 circular with Hines's black-and-white line drawings and flyway maps. Nevertheless, the GPO sold over one hundred thousand copies of the publication at thirty cents apiece. Hines revealed in a letter to Paul Brooks that Doubleday & Company later "reprinted it in its entirety, save for cover and title page, and issued it in a hardback copy and charged a dollar a copy." As the material remained in the public domain, "they pocketed all the profits themselves. . . . Mr. Lincoln told me that at one time Doubleday had sold more dollar copies than the government had ever printed." One review of the Doubleday edition states, "Aimed at the pocket book trade, the little volume is of course cheaply gotten out. Reduction to pocket size has left the print still legible, but has robbed the dramatic picto-maps by Bob Hines of much of their clarity and detail." Full-color Hines illustrations further enliven a 1979 revised edition of the booklet. Dan Saults, one of Hines's colleagues at the Service, complimented the book: "Bird paintings by Bob Hines, himself a classic, adorn the cover and give life to the simplified sketch maps of migration that complement the text. Those paintings glow with color, almost movement."

Bob received a $500 bonus for his work on the revised *Migration of Birds*. A memorandum in Hines's personnel file supports his contribution to the publication: "The task of redesigning and illustrating the new book was given to Bob Hines, National Wildlife Artist. This additional project, on top of a schedule already filled with tight deadlines for art needed in other projects, created a serious logistical problem for Mr. Hines. Consequently, he was forced to spend many hours beyond his normal work schedule . . . on this revision, which the Government Printing Office was anxious to receive for use in responding to the many requests and inquiries for sales copies of this book. [It] is approaching the status of a [GPO] 'best seller,' reflecting both its popularity and its quality." The memo concludes, "Not only does this successful publication add prestige to the professional quality of work produced at the US Fish and Wildlife Service, but it provides the ultimate fulfillment of our obligation to the American public. . . . In view of the numerous demands on his time, Bob Hines' excellence in accomplishing this project merits recognition, and a cash award is authorized."

As Hines acquired seniority within the Service, he reached a ceiling at a GS rating of 14, his lack of higher education preventing a further promotion beyond his title of visual information officer. Bob strived to be cordial to his boss, John Mattoon, despite a mutual dislike between the two men. When the opportunity for a promotion arose in the Information Office, Mattoon advanced Hines's colleague. To appease Hines, Mattoon bestowed the title of "National Wildlife Artist" on Bob. Hines, whose metric of success was strictly financial, remained unappreciative: "Here doggie, here's a bone. That's what it amounted to."

Human activities began to affect the remote landscape of Alaska. In 1958 an outcry from the Native people curtailed a proposed peaceful use of atomic energy to blast a deep water harbor along the Chukchi Sea coastline at Cape Thompson. Federal officials executed three subterranean nuclear detonations on Amchitka Island near the western end of the Aleutian Island chain between 1965 and 1971. Elsewhere, aggressive dredging of waterways fouled salmon streams. With the completion of the trans-Alaska oil pipeline in 1977, staff members at the US FWS Regional Office in Anchorage expressed concerns about the threat of a possible oil spill to the richness of the state's coastal wildlife. Bill Reffalt, chief of Alaskan refuges for the Service, petitioned the Information Service to promote those species of wildlife at risk to human interference. Hines readily accepted an assignment to return to Alaska, one of his favorite destinations, spending three weeks during the summer of 1978 traveling from the wooded southeast corner of the state through the Aleutians and on to the Pribilof Islands. Bob visited Chisik Island within Cook Inlet where pine martins leave their forest habitat to prey on nesting eider ducks and their ducklings along the coast with its sparse cover of dwarf willow.

Hines traveled in a reconfigured Gruman Goose aircraft; its high wing profile allowed unobstructed window views of the cliffs and sea stacks along the Bering Sea coastline. Bob reported that he had spent his time in Alaska, "sketching, listening, and learning." Service colleague Clay Hardy did not remember Hines either photographing or sketching, just soaking up the details of the unique landscape into his memory. Bob was eager to reunite with Bob "Sea Otter" Jones, with whom he spent over two weeks during his 1954 visit to Cold Bay. That remote area of the state supported the entire world's population of black brant. Hines also observed the Peale's subspecies of peregrine falcon, a darker form of the northwest, capturing auklets in flight. "In the Aleutians, to see [the falcon] come out like an apparition out of the fog, this black arrow . . . looks like a peregrine except he is so black, so dark really, that at a distance he looks black." Hardy accompanied Hines on a fishing trip at Ugashik Narrows. Bob was displeased with his own lack of success, largely because of his inability to cast a fishing line any distance.

From Anchorage, Hines traveled with Jo Keller, an FWS photographer, to St. Paul, one of the Pribilof Islands. They departed in an Electra two-engine prop airplane. The aircraft swept gently just above the waves in order to locate the island because of the poor weather. Upon their arrival, Jo and Bob stayed in a small hotel with shared bathrooms. On the island, they observed colonies of seabirds in noisy thousands. Hines elaborated, "To see those birds up there, they can darken the sky when they take off from the cliffs. The murres are black on the back and white [on the] belly, like penguins almost. When they're sitting on their eggs they have their backs to the sea and their belly to the cliff. You make a loud noise out there and, all of a sudden, they all turn around . . . and the cliff is white now." St. Paul also hosted a spectacle of kittiwakes by the thousands, pelagic gulls that come ashore only to breed. When an eagle approaches, it becomes "completely surrounded by screaming kittiwakes, dive bombing him and blasting him and everything else. When I made the painting I couldn't paint it that way, because it would not have shown the eagle. I had to show it being chased." The kittiwakes coexist with ravens on these seaside cliffs. When the kittiwakes left their nest to mob an eagle, it was the raven that slipped in and quietly preyed on the kittiwake eggs or young.

Hines could not participate in the Federal Duck Stamp contest as an employee of the Service. During his talks with Keller, Bob revealed a determination to enter the competition after his forthcoming retirement. He was intrigued with the harlequin duck, a denizen of these rough waters of the northwest, feeling that a design had not yet adequately portrayed that species on past stamps. Walking along the rugged terrain of the Pribilofs, Hines recalled that Jo Keller would, "take the darnest chances. She'd stand right on the ragged edge of nothing and take pictures out there. I knew she was going to die, but she didn't." Puffins and auklets would land close to the sitting humans. Hines privately wished he had lived in a prior century when he could have experienced America as an untouched wilderness: "There were foxes and reindeer on the island. It was a wonderful place to be." Alaska's pristine beauty satisfied this anachronistic fantasy.

Prior to Hines's departure for Alaska, he confessed that he was developing some balance issues and an unsteady gait. After acclimating himself to the precipitous landscape along the Alaskan coast, he confidently scaled an extension ladder upon his arrival home to paint the second-floor dormer windows of his house. Bob spent about a year's time on his Alaskan portfolio, after which he returned to Anchorage, this time with his wife Nancy, for a critique of his artwork. Bob never saw a pine martin on Chisik Island. When he inquired about the appearance of the creature, his colleagues described it as a mink with a bushy tail. Hines's rendition of the martin had an exaggeratedly full tail, which he corrected. Many of the staff members present were in awe of Hines and, therefore, reluctant to offer any meaningful suggestions. Clay Hardy was annoyed that his Service colleagues were free with their criticism in Hines's absence. Had they been forthright with their comments, Hines could have corrected any errors. Some of the pieces have a loose, amateurish quality to them with poor perspective, certainly not befitting a National Wildlife Artist of Hines's stature. Inexplicably, some of these lesser quality renditions became part of the portrait series, "A Host of Seabirds—Alaska." The six-print series sold for $5. Bob recalled, "[T]he paintings were supposed to tell the story of the value of the resource we have up there. [The series] didn't gain as much publicity as they had hoped." Sadly, the initial concerns of an oil spill along the Alaskan coast did come to fruition later with the 1989 Exxon Valdez accident in Prince William Sound.

In addition to Hines's duties at the Service, he led an active avocation as a freelance artist. Bob admitted, "Pencils are easy. I like to use soft pencils and made good drawings. I seem to have hit a pattern that can reproduce really well in a book and makes it easy to do." He was also equally adept at pen-and-ink drawings. His clean line illustrations enhance a number of books on which he collaborated with such noted authors as Sigurd Olson, Peter Matthiesen, Isaac Azimov, and Peter Farb. Hines's more scientific works include Watson's *Birds of the Antarctic and Subantarctic* (1975) and Bellrose's *Ducks, Geese, and Swans of North America* (1980).

Dr. George Watson, curator of birds at the Smithsonian Museum, interceded so that Bob could use the facility's collection of study skins for his research for the Antarctic guide. Watson was chagrined at a minor error in the color plates upon the book's release. One keen reviewer, who tested the manuscript on an Antarctic cruise, detected Hines's shortcoming: "How I wanted to tell artist Bob Hines not to use large pupils in the eyes of his penguins, for even in fairly poor light the pupils of most penguins seen by us appeared as pinpoints, giving the penguin its colorful but blank, pupilless appearing eye." The review concluded, "The black-and-white illustrations play their role well, but it is the color plates that one will return to time and again throughout one's voyage. Composites showing many birds in flight are a difficult, dreary proposition for any artist. Bob Hines is to be congratulated for pulling it off as well as he has, for his was an especially tough assignment with so many birds with similar shapes and colors."

Not all of Hines's projects came to fruition. Undated photographs from his files show Bob at the drawing board preparing color plates for *LeMoyne's Bird Dictionary*. A signed 1965 contract with Doubleday & Company documents proposed twenty-five black-and-white drawings and ten four-color paintings for *The Cats: From Tigers and Cheetahs to Common House Cats* with Hines's colleague Will Barker as the author.

The African Safari Club of Washington was an elite group of affluent members who shared an interest in preserving the wildlife of Africa. The officers contracted Hines to complete a series of oil paintings that were given annually to a worthy figure in international conservation. Bob was especially pleased when his artwork went to honor two US Fish and Wildlife directors: John Gottschalk received a painting of nyalas in 1979, while Lynn Greenwalt received a painting of two cheetahs the following year. Hines enjoyed attending the club's annual Conservation Award Dinner as its well-heeled members treated him graciously. Bob appreciated the adulation that he received outside his government circle. He began to entertain thoughts of retiring from the Service so that he could freely pursue the projects of his own choosing.

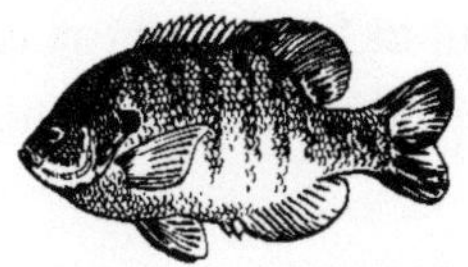

Chapter 10

Senescence

Bob Hines was totally committed to his craft as a wildlife artist, which he felt was a higher calling with a concomitant urgency to translate his mental images onto paper or canvas. Some career bureaucrats at the Interior Department incorrectly interpreted his sense of mission as arrogance, an exaggerated sense of self-importance. To avoid the morning rush hour traffic of Washington, Bob would arrive early at the Interior Building where he would first visit the cafeteria for coffee and breakfast. When Tom Duncan presented Hines a miniature carved goose call, Bob demonstrated its effectiveness freely, the acoustics echoing off the walls of the cafeteria, much to the annoyance of other patrons. Hines would ascend to the north penthouse where he would cloister himself in his studio.

Though Hines may have groused at the inertia of government work, Phil Million, who occupied an office in the north penthouse adjacent to Hines's studio, recalls that Bob never complained about his role as staff artist for the Service. With a strong work ethic, Hines frequently would work through his lunch hour, prioritizing the multiple requests for assignments he received from across the country. The Information Office also fielded questions from the general public. Handling those telephone calls provided equal measures of amusement and aggravation for Bob. He shared with a journalist, "I get my inspiration from daydreaming. I'm always thinking about the whales in the ocean or the birds in my backyard. I can see them in my mind." During any meetings Bob attended, he would frequently doodle on his papers, tossing them into the wastebasket as he exited the room. In time, his impromptu sketches became collector's items as his colleagues salvaged them from the trash can.

As a diversion, Hines once made arrangements to go turkey hunting with his friend, Aelred Geis. They launched a small boat headed for an island near the Maryland side of the Potomac River. In the solitude of that early morning dawn, Al's turkey calls attracted four gobblers in the vicinity. Bob had his twelve-gauge shotgun with its 30" barrel at the ready. As he fired at one turkey, aiming at its head, the bird instinctively crouched down, pivoted its foot in the soft soil, and flew directly away from the hunter. After quiet returned following the gunshot, Geis plaintively informed Hines, "Well, you missed him." During Bob's oral history, he chortled, "I think that's the most obvious statement [I] ever heard." Back at the office, Hines reported his embarrassment. The story of his missing a turkey at thirteen yards became an oft-repeated tale around the Service watercoolers.

Approaching seventy years of age, Bob had advanced in the government hierarchy as far as he could to chief, Office of Audiovisual, at a general schedule grade of 14 with a salary of $41,655. After more than three decades in the federal government, he decided to retire from the Service effective March 1980. However, he continued on for another year as a reemployed annuitant at a salary of $45,443. Hines's pending retirement became a featured story in the Fremont and Washington newspapers as well as one magazine with an international distribution. The latter referred to Bob as "the eye of the nation when it comes to wildlife." Hines's colleagues feted him with a party held in the Interior Department cafeteria, "a not-so-wildlife sendoff" according to a blurb in the *Washington Post*.

Upon his official retirement in 1981, Hines received congratulatory letters from across the country. Outgoing Interior Secretary Cecil Andrus described Bob as "one of the great people in the Interior Department—a standout in a wonderfully talented crowd." Service Director Lynn Greenwalt recalled how Hines's clip art could enhance government reports, "adding luster to basically lusterless stuff." Greenwalt continued, "Bob Hines always has been a person who never let the organization down. He has been a strong supporter of the organization and of the conservation movement. And, unlike many of the rest of us, he has had a singular talent to make his message get across. He can bring animals to life on paper and canvas and for those of us who know something about the out-of-doors and how valuable it is to the Nation, he can make those pictures breathe and sing for us. For the layman he achieves much the same thing, but perhaps without the passion and fervor that comes to those of us who have come away from the reality of the field into the somewhat unreal world of the office." Greenwalt predicted Hines's "legacy is a real one and will live on for a very, very long time. Your absence from this building will touch us all very soon and life will not be the same for us."

Bea Boone shared that she would miss beginning her work day with the greeting, "Good morning, Mr. Hines," a routine she had practiced for fifteen years.

Arthur Hawkins revealed, "I can't imagine you in retirement. I suspect it will be a ceremonial event, an interlude as you shift gears." Hawkins concluded, "Few people in the wildlife biz have made a bigger splash than you have. You have left footprints—big ones—all over the place."

Similarly, Thomas Duncan wrote, "When I heard that you had decided to retire, my first reaction was . . . 'He's not retiring, he's aspiring'—and I felt much better."

Phil Million contributed, "It's going to be hard to adjust to your absence behind the easel in the North Penthouse. The talent you exercised there and the beautiful products that flowed from it will never be duplicated or replaced. Your departure impoverishes not only the Fish and Wildlife Service, but all of us who remain in this department." Million addressed Hines's "unfailing good counsel," "encyclopedic knowledge of wildlife," and "ability to produce art of the highest caliber under conditions that were often less than ideal."

Bob's supervisor, John Mattoon, pondered, "How does one say farewell to a living legend? [T]here will be a real void and emptiness in Public Affairs and the Service. They say artists are a different kind of people, and quite well they should be. To be able to express with such beauty the natural wonders of the wildlife world is indeed a talent and vocation that very few possess. The work you have done for the Service and people of this country will long be remembered and cherished. . . . The Service will not be the same without your contributions, for you cannot be replaced."

Perhaps the most touching letter was from octogenarian Mary Williams handwritten in a neatly controlled cursive. Miss Williams was Bob's former art teacher from Fremont who gave him his four-day refresher art course before he began his career with the Ohio Division of Conservation and Natural Resources in 1938. She wrote, "To have you share with me a knowledge of your honors and achievements has always been one of my greatest joys. . . . You have always had great talent and I am very pleased that, in a very small way, I had the opportunity to help you develop that ability."

Bob himself revealed in a letter, "I still spend lotsa [sic] time painting ~ now it's mostly what I want to paint instead of what some bureaucrat thinks I should." Hines began to capitalize on his former title by signing letters as "National Wildlife Artist, Retired."

Upon his retirement from the Service, he began two notable partnerships. Because of his ties to Ohio, Bob became acquainted with Bill and Elsa Thompson, who were launching *Bird Watcher's Digest* from their hometown of Marietta. Hines composed the cover artwork that appeared on eight issues of the magazine. He also illustrated *Stories About Birds and Bird-watchers*, Mary Beacon Bowers's 1981 collection of birding essays from the *Digest*. One reviewer noted, "The illustrations, which are first-rate, are by a bird watcher named Bob Hines. He has been paying attention." On his file copy of the review, Hines underlined the reference to him in red pencil, adding the notation, "Amen!"

Bob maintained a respect for conservation efforts at the grass roots level. Through the intercession of colleague Jim Miller, Hines agreed to create an award for volunteer leaders of the National 4-H Wildlife and Fisheries program. Each year, Miller queried the six nationally recognized individuals as to their favorite species of wildlife. Bob then painted a watercolor image of that creature along with a hand-lettered personalized inscription for each recipient. The tradition persisted for a full decade, with Hines's service being gratis. An inspection of the later pieces reveal a slight loss in the precision of Bob's printing.

One personal goal that eluded Hines was his ambition to compose a second winning Federal Duck Stamp design. Emboldened with his 1975

Abercrombie & Fitch National Fish Stamp, and later a 1982 Virginia Wild Turkey Stamp, Bob was free as a private citizen to submit entries to the competition after his retirement from the Service and his professional involvement with the Federal Duck Stamp contest.

The character of the Duck Stamp competition changed with the death of Bea Boone, Bob's former assistant, in 1982. Columnist James Bruns devoted a portion of his weekly "Stamps and Coins" feature to report Boone's death from a liver ailment at age sixty-seven. "The limelight seldom shines on those who work behind the scenes. That certainly is true about one person who worked diligently for years on the Interior Department's annual duck stamp design competition." Bruns added, "She was sort of the government's assurance against some little thing going wrong."

With Hines's departure, Pete Anastasi returned out of retirement to coordinate the Duck Stamp contest. Bob cheekily recorded his heartfelt wish: "Retirement has shown me another perspective. I was on the inside for over 30 years. Now . . . I have become one of the entrants, and some day—yeah, some day—the phone just might ring, and Pete will say, 'Hey, Amigo . . . you better sit down to hear this."

As the art form evolved to include unique eye-catching angles and colorful backlighting, Hines's traditional style and a faltering dexterity conspired against him. Bob recalled: "[O]ver the years I had an amazing 50 percent selection of winners. [Y]et, since then when I've tried to enter, I have [had] zero won. My entries don't get anywhere. I can't draw one that gets the same reception. But when I do and if I do, you will have to hold your ears because I'm going to yell out loud, real loud."

Notwithstanding Hines's disappointment for a second Duck Stamp design, he remained a member of the program's storied history. In 1984, Bob accepted an invitation to attend a Rose Garden ceremony at the White House in which President Ronald Reagan signed a proclamation that distinguished "National Duck Stamp Week" during the "Golden Anniversary Year of the Duck Stamp."

Hines channeled his energies toward opportunities as a freelance artist. He accepted several invitations to judge at regional wildlife art or waterfowl carving competitions. As the artist in residence, Bob frequently would donate his paintings completed at the event as an award presented to the top craftsman. One particularly generous donation was an oil painting of an Alaskan bull moose to a raffle benefiting the Coonskin Cap Brigade, an offshoot organization of the League of Ohio Sportsmen, which instructs youth on shooting sports and outdoor activities. A notice of the raffle with its one dollar ticket price states, "Appraised value of this original oil by the famous Ohio artist is $5,000."

Sometimes Hines collaborated with authors whom he never met, such as the enigmatic Isaac Asimov, whose book, *Ends of the Earth: The Polar Regions of the World*, Hines illustrated.

Bob developed friendships with other collaborating authors, such as George Reiger. Bob's pencil drawings complement Reiger's 1983 release, *Wanderer on My Native Shore*, an ecological account of wildlife along the mid-atlantic seaboard. Reiger appreciated Hines's collaboration, believing that Hines could capture mood and tone well in his drawings, perhaps even better than with his painting. One autumn, Reiger invited Hines and Pete Anastasi on a hunting trip to the Eastern Shore of Virginia, that spur of land surrounded by the Atlantic Ocean to the east and by the Chesapeake Bay to the west. Grayson Chesser led the men by boat to Assawoman Island, one of a necklace of barrier islands along the Atlantic coastline of Virginia. A thick fog blanketed the area, creating an aura of mystery as the small boat departed for its unseen destination. Once on the island, the men's quarry was migrating snow geese, the white plumage of which appeared ghostly in the persistent haze. A previous fall on the front porch at home resulted in an injury of Hines's right shoulder that required surgical intervention for a muscle tear. Unfortunately, Bob's subsequent reduced arm mobility presented a handicap while hunting. Reiger's shot hit a snow goose that disappeared in the fog. Chesser's trusty retriever located the missing bird and dutifully returned it to the hunting party. Anastasi was shocked to learn that the goose he bagged bore a radio transmitter. After returning home, Pete submitted the identification information; he was relieved to learn from waterfowl researchers that the transmitter had malfunctioned. With Pete's input, the data bank acquired additional facts on the movement of the tagged bird.

Chesser had encamped in an area fringed with phragmites, the tall reeds providing a filter for the gusty coastal winds. After supper and a night cap, Hines, Anastasi, and Reiger fell asleep early that evening. Later as Chesser joined them in the tent, Hines began to moan loudly as though he were in pain. Grayson's mind raced in an effort to determine how he could evacuate the afflicted guest off this remote island. Hines shouted, "Buck Rogers, you go to hell!" In his restlessness, Bob sidled across both cots. Buck Rogers had been a comic strip space explorer who was the subject of a radio show that later transitioned to early television in the middle decades of the last century. Chesser awakened the distraught Hines, questioning why he was dreaming about a fictional character. Bob lucidly recalled that E. L. "Buck" Rogers, the past president of the Outdoor Writers Association of America, was a former colleague with whom he had had a running feud.

Hines's physical health began a slow, steady decline around the time of his retirement from the Service. "Cigar" Daisey recalled that Bob tripped and fell while judging at the 1987 Ward Championship competition in Salisbury, Maryland. When Daisey came to his aid and asked him if he was hurt, Hines replied, "I'm not hurt, just embarrassed."

As Bob aged, he began to criticize other drivers in an impatient, short-tempered manner. Hines's companions on outdoor excursions refused to be passengers with Bob behind the wheel. They instinctively offered to drive, allowing Hines to be their guest, who contributed to the travel expenses. Bob's personal emphasis on hunting changed from blood sports to an enjoyment of camaraderie, fellowship, and food. George Reiger recalled that while hunting for mourning doves, Hines's inability to raise and fire his shotgun prompted him to wander voluntarily about the fields as a living scarecrow, thereby keeping the doves in flight to the advantage of other hunters.

With a 1989 Christmas card, Bob shared, "My own [career] is winding down—but is not dead. Main problem is arthritis, which puts a crimp in a guy's enthusiasm." He then revealed, "No hunting—I take so many pratfalls (arthritis again) that I'd endanger everyone, even if the gun would be on safe. But fishing—Ah! I can sit on my duff and haul in the bluegills & bass and enjoy, which is what I did."

Hines's last major commission was an assignment to illustrate a fiftieth anniversary edition of Rachel Carson's first book, *Under the Sea-wind,* for a 1991 release. Although Bob may have felt sentimental regarding the project because of his past friendship and collaboration with Carson, the publisher's motive was strictly economic. Truman Talley, executive of his eponymous printing house, bluntly queried Hines: "Please call me sometime after Easter and let me know how many 'vista' and 'spot' illustrations you think a 50th anniversary edition of the book should have and what your fee will come to. Since revivals are often risky, please give me your best, i.e. rock-bottom, figure!" As Hines aged, he developed an unsteady hand, the bane of an artist. Bob's daughter Nancy recalls that it took longer for him to complete the pencil drawings for this project than it would have in previous years. The resulting illustrations lack Hines's precise draftsmanship from his work on *The Edge of the Sea*. However, this lighter touch creates a simplicity that complements the volume. In a final request from a family friend, Bob hand-colored over fifty prints of a rising mallard drake as a gift to opponents of a water project in North Dakota. The members of this select group with their diverse backgrounds surreptitiously referred to themselves as "the Secret Order of the Mallards."

The US Fish and Wildlife Service began to examine its contributions to the evolving discipline of environmental history. By early 1991, Hines, along with his trusted friend Pete Anastasi, agreed to a detailed interview of their employment in the Service. This commitment stretched into multiple sessions that encompass ten hours of videotape documentation. Bob's knack as a raconteur is evident in the footage and its transcript. Hines appears lucid with fluid speech, occasionally blocking on a name that he may not have thought of in years. Bob displayed a philosophical side when he reported that Amos Berg, a photographer with *National Geographic* on assignment in Alaska, shared with Hines his thought-provoking maxim: "God never worried about what kind of package you put a soul in." Bob commented: "There are times in my life when I hated people for one characteristic or another. . . . [T]hey got as much right to be what they are as I have to be me. [Berg's comment] is very beautiful. [I]f you use it, you will have a better life. It has helped me." With a more titillating answer, Hines later reveals that he had a three-year affair with a noted burlesque dancer. "I've been to her home, but it wasn't to paint. It was extracurricular and before I was married." Bob's clarification, likely uttered within earshot of wife Nancy, was misleading and disingenuous. The affair occurred while he was still married to Edna Hines.

Bob's decades of cigarette smoking began to affect his breathing. He consulted three psychologists to aid him in overcoming this vice. His wife Nancy

H. Hines continued to smoke, exposing Bob to second-hand tobacco smoke. When he developed insomnia, Bob started having a nightcap to help him fall asleep. Nancy projected that he was "pickling his nerves" by abusing alcohol. Nancy began her own personal decline when she resumed her drinking. As Bob's health weakened, the thirteen-year age difference between the two spouses became evident. Unwilling to care for her ailing husband, Nancy decided to place Bob in an assisted living facility until his condition further deteriorated to require skilled nursing care. At this point, Nancy filed papers for a legal separation, the preliminary step in obtaining a divorce. Bob's nursing home bills drained the couple's finances. Together, they owed $17,000 on their house mortgage in addition to a home equity mortgage of $27,000. The legal settlement agreement granted ownership to Bob of "all paintings created by him, a marble clock, and certain first edition illustrated wildlife books." Nancy acquired sole possession of the house, Bob's Social Security and Civil Service retirement benefits with a combined monthly total of $4,000, Bob's Prudential life insurance policy, and the couple's 1988 Chevrolet. There was a financial benefit to Nancy's usurpation of assets in that Bob would consequently qualify for Medicaid coverage of his nursing home expenses.

Debra Berke visited Hines in the nursing home for an interview prior to the opening of a Bob Hines display at the Interior Department's museum in 1991. She found him tearful because of his recent divorce proceedings. As a man who measured his success in financial terms, Bob desperately told Berke that he had to enter the Duck Stamp competition so that he could earn some money. Bob was able to attend the opening reception of the exhibit in his wheelchair. Former Service Director John Gottschalk praised Hines's career as "the work of the man who will go down in conservation annals as the ultimate government fish and wildlife artist." Gottschalk added: "Those of us who are fortunate enough to have an original 'Hines' consider it a treasure, both for the art and for the story it tells." He artfully concluded his speech with the remark, "It is not difficult to evaluate the significance of Bob's contributions to the American conservation movement. Happily they exemplify Shakespeare's well known comment: 'There is a tide in the affairs of men, which, taken at the flood, leads on to fortune.' We are here today to recognize both the tide that brought Bob Hines to the conservation movement, and this excellent exhibition of his work." Visitors to the event noted

Bob's emotional lability. Hines autographed a copy of *Sport Fishing USA*. His signature, once executed with such artistic flair, was a barely legible scrawl. Collectors approached Pete Anastasi requesting Hines's signature on their stamps or prints. Pete assured the collectors that should he approach Bob with their requests, they would not be able to read Hines's inscription.

Daughter Nancy Hines accompanied her father as he appeared before a nursing home panel. She recalls with pride that Hines identified himself as "I am Bob Hines, artist." He became increasingly frail medically with a diminished appetite and a need for supplemental oxygen as his lungs deteriorated. A chronic diarrhea racked Hines's already lean body. Pete exceeded his role as a friend by changing Bob's soiled adult diapers during visits to the nursing home. John Gottschalk and his wife Edith likewise visited Hines. Edith, who trained as a nurse, would rub Bob's feet to relax him. She recalled that he would lament, "I wish I could love [wife] Nancy." During those long, lonely days, Hines punished himself for being an absent father to his children. As an artist, Bob imbued his subjects with such vitality; now he felt his own life force ebbing away.

Bob Hines died at eighty-two years of age on November 6, 1994, from a pneumonia superimposed on his chronic lung disease. Russell Fink called Nancy H. Hines to convey his condolences after learning of Bob's death. Fink was unprepared when Nancy, who at the time was apparently inebriated, spat, "I'm glad the son of a bitch is dead!"

Daughter Nancy dabbled in art, having studied block printing in Japan. For sentimental reasons, she wanted her father's well-used drawing board, riddled with innumerable thumb tack holes. When daughter Nancy approached her former stepmother, she was dismayed to learn that the drawing board had disappeared along with the premium pieces of her father's artwork. Daughter Nancy hastily assembled a collection of remnants and discards that were poorly representative of her father's artistic output. As daughter Nancy returned to her automobile, clutching the last tangible link to her father, Nancy H. Hines thoughtlessly screamed, "How much money do you think you will get for those?"

Nancy H. Hines made no arrangements for a public funeral service, no obituary in the newspapers. Colleague V. Daniel Stiles noted in an interoffice US Fish and Wildlife Service memo that Hines's "practiced eye could see incredible details in a sunset or the breast feather of a wild turkey." Bob's cremains returned to his home state, distributed around a venerable white oak tree that towers under Ohio skies. A small, gray granite marker bears a reproduction of Bob Hines's clear signature with the simple inscription, "Artist. 1912–1994."

With the advent of the Internet, Hines has achieved technological immortality with several online versions of "Ducks at a Distance." An examination of Bob Hines's life and accomplishments offers a glimpse of the history of the conservation movement in the past century. Bob Hines left behind an incredible body of work, a visual legacy that allows each person to connect with the natural world that Hines understood and cherished.

Epilogue

As an unenlightened youth, Aldo Leopold, the future dean of ecology and land management, believed that fewer predators had to translate into more deer for the sportsman. In his essay, "Thinking Like a Mountain," Leopold documents an early experience while hunting wolves that drastically changed his human-centered logic. After Leopold's hunting party fired into a pack of wolves, he "reached the old wolf in time to watch a fierce green fire dying in her eyes." In that moment, Leopold observed not only the death of the animal but also the demise of that ineffable quality of wildness. The role of predators in the ecological fabric of the landscape manifested itself with sobering clarity. The essay concludes, "Perhaps this is behind Thoreau's dictum: In wildness is the salvation of the world. Perhaps this is the hidden meaning in the howl of a wolf, long known among mountains, but seldom perceived among men."

The final sentence can serve as an epitaph for Bob Hines, the only US National Wildlife Artist, whose innate talent enabled him to translate his unique perception of the natural world, along with the idiosyncrasies of his subjects, into artwork that continues to enlighten, inspire, and educate the general public about a realm that predates humankind itself.

References

Chapter 1

Hines, Bob, "A Winter's Visit to Brady's Island," *Fremont Daily News* (January 15, 1927): 2.

Hines, Murray J., *The Genealogy of John and Mary (Roderick) Hines: A One Family Study* (Unpublished, 2007). I remain grateful to Murray Hines for his generosity in sharing with me his thorough genealogy of the John Hines and Mary Roderick family history.

Weiss, Michael J., "Bob Hines: A Wild Artist," *American Way* (May 1981): 105–9.

Biographical and Historical Memoirs of Muskingum County, Ohio (Chicago: Goodspeed Publishers, 1892), 466. (Nathaniel Hines, 1803–1886; Delilah Brelsford Hines, 1799–1871).

The Household Guide and Instructor with Biographies. History of Guernsey County, Ohio. (Cleveland: T. F. Williams, 1882), 547.

"Anniversary Notice," *Sandusky Star* (June 13, 1891).

"Engineer Seber Killed at Hancock Street Crossing," *Sandusky Daily Star* (August 28, 1900).

"Coroner's Verdict Is that Motorman Hines Was Criminally Careless," *Sandusky Daily Star* (September 1, 1900).

"Made Public Is News of Indictment of N. W. Hines," *Sandusky Daily Star* (September 28, 1900).

"Not Guilty Is the Verdict in the Hines Case," *Sandusky Daily Star* (November 16, 1900).

"To an Assignee: Mrs. Hines Deeds the Waldorf," *Sandusky Daily Star* (February 19, 1901).

"The Waldorf: Some Facts about the Assignment—Unfortunate Circumstances," *Sandusky Daily Star* (February 20, 1901).
"The Social Chronicle: Society Gossip of the Day," *Sandusky Daily Star* (September 18, 1901). Nathan Hines and wife move to Columbus.
"A Year in Andersonville Prison Was the Experience of N. W. Hines who Died Tuesday in Leesburg Township," *Marysville Evening Tribune* (June 12, 1907): 2.
"Obituary: Nathan W. Hines," *Delaware Semi-weekly Gazette* (June 12, 1907): 6.
"Records of the Day," *Columbus Evening Dispatch* (February 17, 1912).
"The Sudden Death of Mrs. G. W. Hines," *Fremont Daily News* (December 24, 1925).
Mabel Elwood Hines. December 24, 1925. Certificate of Death. State of Ohio, Department of Health, Division of Vital Statistics.
"Old Fashioned Runaway Attracts Lots of Attention: Team's Mad Rampage," *Fremont News Messenger* (December 21, 1926).
"Honors in Scoutdom Awarded the Winners," *Fremont Daily News* (February 8, 1929).
"Fame Flames in Fremont: R. W. Hines Designs New Wildlife Stamp," *Toledo Sunday Blade* (March 2, 1958): 1.
"American Civil War Regiments, 122nd Infantry Regiment Ohio, Date of Organization October 1, 1862; Muster date June 26, 1865." www.ancestry.com database (1999).
1880 Census, New Concord, Union Township, Muskingum County, Ohio.
Marriage Record (September 10, 1907), Probate Court, Franklin County, Ohio. George Warren Hines and Mable [sic] Nunemacher.
1920 Census, Franklin County, 16th Ward, Ohio.
Certificate of Death. Mabel Elwood Hines. State of Ohio, Department of Health, Division of Vital Statistics. Date of Death December 24, 1925.
The Croghan, 1928. Fremont (Ohio) High School yearbook.
Bob Hines/Pete Anastasi Oral History (1991). US Fish and Wildlife Service, National Conservation Training Center (BH/PA OH). Tapes 5–8 and 25–28.
Interview with Bobbie Hines Blowers (June 8, 2009).
Interview with anonymous Hines relative (NH) (July 31, 2010). George W. Hines told his sons and grandchildren about an Irish connection in

the Hines ancestry. Death of Mary Ann Hines. Details of Bob Hines's boyhood.

I thank Stephanie Evans of Schoedinger Funeral Service, Columbus, Ohio, for this information: Mary Ann Hines, born August 15, 1916; died August 16, 1916. Kathy Marine later located a copy of the death certificate.

I am especially indebted to George and Virginia Nunemacher, Columbus, Ohio, for providing me with photographs of Mabel Nunemacher Hines.

The street addresses of the Hines's residences in Fremont were 814 Napoleon Street and then 716 West State Street. The latter address appears in the 1931 Fremont directory.

The *Wildlife Management* Boy Scout merit badge handbook includes a reprint of the food chain illustration from the *Nature* merit badge handbook.

Chapter 2

Hines, Bob, "Snakes of Ohio: Paging St. Patrick," *The Ohio Conservation Bulletin* (June 1945): 16–17.

——, "Panorama of a 'Hun' Hunt," *The Ohio Conservation Bulletin* (October 1945): 12–13.

Stone, John Cary, "Robert Hines: Painter to the Nation's Vanishing First Families," *The Washington Post, Potomac* (January 31, 1971): 25.

Weiss, Michael J., "Bob Hines: A Wild Artist," *American Way* (May 1981): 107.

Welles, Edward O., Jr., "The Wildlife of Bob Hines," *The Washington Post Magazine* (April 27, 1980): 42.

"The Editor's Page," *The Ohio Conservation Bulletin* (April 1941): 2.

Uncredited cover photos of Hines, *The Ohio Conservation Bulletin* (November 1941 and September 1943): Front covers.

Impending encounter between skunk and dogs, *The Ohio Conservation Bulletin* (November 1945): Front cover.

"They Swim, They Walk but the Air Is Their True Element," *The Ohio Conservation Bulletin* (January 1947).

Fourth of July raccoons, *The Ohio Conservation Bulletin* (July 1947): Front cover.

"Ed Dodd's Felicitations," *The Ohio Conservation Bulletin* (September 1948): 1.
"Plan to Attend the Ohio State Fair," *The Ohio Conservation Bulletin* (August 1950): 8.
"Mary Williams," [obituary] *Fremont News Messenger* (March 8, 1991). Miss Williams (1898–1991) earned her bachelor's degree in education and her master's degree in art from Ohio University. She taught art in the Fremont public schools from 1923 to 1962.
1934 Flastacowo [yearbook]. The Florida State College for Women. Tallahassee, Florida.
BH/PA OH. Tapes 1–4 and 25–28.
Bob Hines Journal (October 1933 – January 1934). I thank William Webster for sharing this document with me.
Robert W. Hines, Application for Federal Employment. National Personnel Records Center, U.S. National Archives and Records Administration (NPRC, NARA).
Record of Marriage Certificate, Robert W. Hines and Edna D. Beatty (April 22, 1939). State of Kentucky, Kenton County Clerk. Copy in the author's collection.
Cross-dressing incident (July 11, 1950). Letter to U.S. Civil Service Commission. Re: Application No. 269028, Announcement U-189. Robert W. Hines. NPRC, NARA.
Thomas O. Duncan Oral History. US Fish and Wildlife Service, National Conservation Training Center (April 21, 2001): 10.
Interview with Pete Anastasi (January 24, 2010).
Interview with Jim McGrady (September 16, 2011).
Photographs of the dioramas are in Hines's personal files.
The mallard duck mural, completed in 1957, now resides in the Bob Hines Conference Room at the Patuxent Research Refuge National Wildlife Visitor's Center in Laurel, Maryland.

Chapter 3

Hartley, Oliver, "High Accomplishment," *The Ohio Conservation Bulletin* (May 1946): 2.
Hines, Bob, "That Lucky 13th Duck Stamp" (1988). Typescript copy from Hines's files.

Minshall, Bob, "Artist Brings Outdoors Home," *The Columbus Sunday Dispatch Magazine* (September 22, 1946): 9.

"1946 Duck Stamp Sales Break Previous Records" (April 3, 1947). Department of the Interior News Release.

BH/PA OH. Tapes 5–8, 13–16, and 25–28.

Letter from J. Hammond Brown to Robert W. Hines (November 10, 1942). Original from Hines's files.

Letter from Albert M. Day to Bob Hines (March 1, 1946). Original letter from Hines's files.

Chapter 4

Bender, Robert W., "Dufresne and Terhune," *Daily Alaska Empire*. NPRC, NARA.

Gray, V. B., "Fly to Lake High in Alaska Peaks," *Cleveland Plain Dealer* (January 8, 1949): 22-A.

Hines, Bob, "That Alaska Trip," *The Ohio Conservation Bulletin* (October 1947): 9.

Hines, Robert W., "Bears Are Just Scenery to Sourdough," *The Columbus Dispatch* (September 24, 1947).

——, "Halibut Head Stew Favorite of Fishers," *The Columbus Dispatch* (September 25, 1947): 1-B.

——, "You See Beaten Salmon in the Spawning Pools," *The Columbus Dispatch* (September 30, 1947): 1-B.

——, "Beautiful Sculpins Will Bite on Anything," *The Columbus Dispatch* (October 1, 1947): 1-B.

——, "Traffic Is Limited on the Alaskan Highway," *The Columbus Dispatch* (October 2, 1947): 1-B.

Stone, John Cary, "Robert Hines: Painter to the Nation's Vanishing First Families," *The Washington Post, Potomac* (January 31, 1971): 25.

Teale, Edwin W., "Alaska's Animals and Fishes, Book Review," *N.Y. Herald Tribune Weekly Book Review* (May 11, 1947): 38.

Weiss, Michael J., "Bob Hines: A Wild Artist," *American Way* (May 1981): 109.

"High Praise for Frank Dufresne," *Outdoors Unlimited* volume 8, number 1 (January 1947): 3.

"Books," *Alaska Life* volume X, number 8 (August 1947): 34. The deluxe edition with a slipcase sold for $15.

"Hines Tells About Alaska," *Wooster Daily Record*. Undated copy [1948] from Hines's files.

The Alaskan Trek News Bulletins No. 1–3 (July 1 & 15, August 1, 1947). Copies in Hines's files.

Frank Dufresne. Application for Employment. U.S. Department of Agriculture. Bureau of Biological Survey (September 12, 1922). NPRC, NARA.

Frank Dufresne. Personal Statement. U.S. Department of Agriculture. Bureau of Biological Survey (December 11, 1922). NPRC, NARA.

Letter from Frank Dufresne to E. W. Nelson (September 22, 1923). NPRC, NARA.

Letter from Frank Dufresne to E. W. Nelson (November 3, 1923). NPRC, NARA.

Letter from E. W. Nelson to Frank Dufresne (August 21, 1924).

Letter from Frank Dufresne to Paul G. Redington (February 1, 1928). NPRC, NARA.

Letter from John Lowell Pratt to BH (March 27, 1947). Original letter in Hines's files.

Memo from Ira Gabrielson to Director of Personnel (April 4, 1944). NPRC, NARA.

BH/PA OH. Tapes 1–4, 17–20, and 29–31.

I thank Russell Fink of Russell Fink Galleries, Lorton, Virginia, for sharing the Rungius and Schaldach inscriptions with me.

Chapter 5

Day, Albert M., "The Problem of Increased Hunting Pressure on Waterfowl" (Speech Transcript, pp. 55–66). *Transactions of the Eleventh North American Wildlife Conference.*

Hines, Robert W., "North with the Ducks," *The Wood Thrush* volume 5, number 3 (January/February 1950): 99–104.

Neal, Harry Edward, *Nature's Guardians: Your Career in Conservation.* (New York: Julian Messner, Inc., 1956): 147.

"Two OWAA Boys Leave Ohio Home Fires," *Outdoors Unlimited* news supplement volume 9 (August 1, 1948): 8.

"Hines Goes Higher," *The Ohio Conservation Bulletin* (August 1948): 2.

"Editorial Bulletin Board," *The Ohio Conservation Bulletin* (April 1949): 2.

"Assorted Comment," *The Ohio Conservation Bulletin* (July 1949): 2.

"A Young Artist of Promise," *The Ohio Conservation Bulletin* (February 1950): 21.

"Please Pardon Our Ego," *The Ohio Conservation Bulletin* (March 1950): 2.

"The Administration: 'The Old Car Peddler,'" *Time* volume LXIV, number 8 (August 23, 1954): 13–18.

Letter from Frank Dufresne to Alastair MacBain (December 7, 1950). Frank Dufresne Federal Personnel File, NPRC, NARA.

Letter from Alastair MacBain to Frank Dufresne (December 15, 1950). Frank Dufresne Federal Personnel File, NPRC, NARA.

Letter from BH to Roger Tory Peterson (December 19, 1955). Roger Tory Peterson Archives, Roger Tory Peterson Institute, Jamestown, New York.

Letter from Robert H. Johnson to Robert W. Hines (March 19, 1957). Robert Hines Federal Personnel File, NPRC, NARA.

Memo from Ira M. Gabrielson to Acting Secretary (March 1, 1946). Albert M. Day Federal Personnel File, U.S. Department of Commerce, National Oceanic and Atmospheric Administration, National Marine Fisheries Service, Seattle, Washington.

Memo from Alastair MacBain to Mr. Conlon (January 27, 1953). "Request for reclassification." Carbon copy in Hines's files. The memo includes an endorsement from FWS Director Al Day: "In a recent interview with the Director on Information activities and personnel, Mr. Day agreed that Bob Hines's value to the Service certainly justified promotion."

Memo from Alastair MacBain to BH (April 2, 1957): "this memorandum will authorize you to give first priority to this assignment, and will relieve you of all other duties for four months from this date to complete those paintings already approved (i.e., winter scene, with mallards; brown bear, [sic] emperor geese and caribou; mountain trout stream fishing scene). Assignment to design and paint murals for halls and offices of Fish and Wildlife Service." Copy from Hines's files. The punctuation error suggests three murals rather than the four that MacBain approved. There is no documentation of the subject change from emperor geese and caribou to commercial tuna fishing.

BH/PA OH. Tapes 1–4 and 17–20.

Frank Dufresne died unexpectedly at seventy years of age on April 10, 1966. Klondy Dufresne (1897–1987) led a colorful life. She moved to Alaska at three years of age when her father entered the Gold Rush. Later, she raised and raced sled dogs. A trained violinist, Klondy offered recitals in culturally starved frontier Alaska.

John Farley Federal Personnel Record. NPRC.

Bill from National Wildlife Federation to BH (April 15, 1956). Six large stamp subjects (beaver dam, raccoon tree, garden planting, hedgerow, marsh management, and farm pond) @ $100. One small stamp subject (fox squirrel) @ $55. Roger Tory Peterson Institute Archives, Jamestown, New York.

1957 stamps: western forest scene, pack train in wilderness area, pumpkinseed, muskalunge [sic], black squirrel. 1958 stamps: otter, chipmunk, thirteen-lined ground squirrel, and antelope jackrabbit. Bills from the National Wildlife Federation to Bob Hines (April 1, 1957, and April 10, 1958, respectively). Roger Tory Peterson Institute Archives, Jamestown, New York.

Chapter 6

Dolin, Eric Jay and Dumaine, B., *The Duck Stamp Story* (Krause Publications: 2000).

Gilmore, Jene C., *Art for Conservation. The Federal Duck Stamps* (Barre, MA: Barre Publishers, 1971), 7. Hines wrote the introduction to this book.

Johnson, Laurence F. *Federal Duck Stamp Story. Fifty Years of Excellence* (Davenport, Iowa: Alexander & Company, 1984).

McBride, David P., *The Federal Duck Stamps: A Complete Guide* (Winchester Press, 1984).

Weidensaul, Scott, *Duck Stamps* (New York City: Gallery Books, 1989).

Hines, Bob, "Some Reminiscences on the Duck Stamp Contest." Undated typescript copy from Hines's files.

——, "Roger Preuss' s claim in the November–December issue of *WILDLIFE ART NEWS* that his 1948 goldeneye design won the first Federal Duck Stamp contest is not true" (December 4, 1989). Typescript copy from Hines's files.

"Decoy Wins Duck Stamp Contest," *Inside Interior* number 3 (October/ November 1974): 8.

"King Eiders Crowned," *Fish and Wildlife News* (November–December 1990): 3.

Letter from BH to Leslie C. Kouba (November 26, 1957). Carbon copy of letter in Hines's files.

Letter from Roger Tory Peterson to Robert Hines (December 4, 1978). Roger Tory Peterson Institute archives.

Memo from E. N. Sater to BH, Frederick Lincoln, and John Aldrich (June 9, 1960). Typescript copy in Hines's files.

"'Duck Stamp' Contest Rules Proposed" (May 3, 1975). Department of the Interior News Release.

"'The Legacy Endures': Smithsonian's Show Tells Story of Waterfowl Conservation, Duck Stamp" (June 9, 1988). Department of the Interior News Release.

Press Release (September 4, 1949). Department of the Interior, Information Service, FWS.

"Honorable mention went to Judy Ellen Wines, age twelve, of Chicago, Illinois" (January 24, 1952). Department of Interior Press Release, Information Service, FWS. Sam Iker corroborates this in "The World's Richest Art Competition," *National Wildlife* (December–January 1979): 43.

BH/PA OH. Tapes 5–8, 9–12, and 13–16.

Beatrice Boone Federal Personnel File, NPRC, NARA.

Interview with Clay Hardy (February 27, 2010).

Federal Duck Stamp website (www.fws.gov/duckstamps).

Chapter 7

Berrill, N. J., "The 'Drama-Filled Fringe,'" *Saturday Review of Literature* (December 3, 1955): 30.

Casteen, Nina, "Book Review," *Library Journal* volume 77 (April 2, 1952): 604.

Martha Freeman (ed.), *Always Rachel. The Letters of Rachel Carson and Dorothy Freeman, 1952-1964.* (Boston: Beacon Press, 1995).

Hines, Bob, "Remembering Rachel," *Yankee* volume 55, number 6 (June 1991): 62–67. I thank *Yankee* magazine for allowing me to quote extensively from Hines's article.

Lear, Linda, *Rachel Carson: Witness for Nature* (New York: Henry Holt, 1997).

"Rhode Plane Wreckage in Alaska Found by Hikers after 21 Years" (September 4, 1979). FWS News Release. See also: Rearden, Jim, "Clarence Rhode" and Miller, Debbie and Dennis, "Finding Clarence Rhode's Plane," *Alaska Magazine* volume XLVI, number 1 (January 1980): 11 and 16 respectively.

"Famous Former Fremonter Is Wildlife Artist," *Fremont News-Messenger* (June 14, 1980).

"There is an air strip at King Salmon. . ." Original photograph with caption in author's possession.

Letter from Paul Brooks (PB) to Rachel Carson (RC) (July 20, 1950). Rachel Carson Papers, Bienecke Rare Book and Manuscript Library, Yale University (RCP).

Letter from RC to PB (July 29, 1950). RCP.

Letter from PB to BH (May 3, 1951). RCP.

Letter from PB to RC (May 5, 1951). RCP.

Letter from RC to PB (May 14, 1951). RCP.

Letter from PB to BH (May 24, 1951). RCP.

Letter from PB to BH (June 6, 1951). RCP.

Letter from BH to PB (June 23, 1951). RCP.

Letter from PB to BH (June 25, 1951). RCP.

Letter from RC to PB (July 7, 1951). RCP.

Letter from BH to PB (July 10, 1951). RCP.

Letter from BH to PB (July 16, 1951). RCP.

Letter from RC to PB (July 16, 1951). RCP.

Letter from RC to PB (December 2, 1951). RCP.

Letter from RC to BH (August 12, 1952). RCP.

Letter from PB to RC (September 3, 1952). RCP.

Letter from BH to PB (September 26, 1952). RCP.

Letter from PB to BH (September 30, 1952). RCP.

Letter from RC to Marie Rodell (MR) (October 1, 1952). RCP.

Letter from PB to RC (January 7, 1953). RCP.

Letter from BH to B. T. Tilghman (BT) (February 20, 1953). RCP. B.T. Tilghman was the production manager of the Houghton Mifflin Trade Department.

Letter from BT to BH (February 24, 1953). RCP.

Letter from PB to RC (February 27, 1953). RCP.

Letter from RC to PB (March 3, 1953). RCP.

Letter from PB to BH (March 10, 1953). RCP.

Letter from MR to PB (March 13, 1953). RCP.

Letter from BH to PB (March 17, 1953). RCP.

Letter from PB to MR (May 7, 1953). RCP.

Letter from Edwin Way Teale to BH (August 23, 1953). Original letter in author's possession.

Letter from RC to BH (August 28, 1953). RCP.

Letter from BH to PB (September 4, 1953). RCP. The book presumably refers to Alexander Klots's *A Field Guide to the Butterflies*, a 1951 release of the HMC Peterson Field Guide Series.

Letter from BH to RC (Undated, circa 1953). RCP.

Letter from BH to PB (April 1, 1954). RCP.

Letter from RC to PB (November 2, 1954). RCP.

Letter from BH to RC (November 6, 1954). Original letter in author's possession.

Letter from RC to PB (April 27, 1955). RCP.

Letter from BH to PB (October 11, 1955). RCP.

Letter from MR to RC (October 11, 1955). RCP.

Letter from Alastair MacBain to PB (October 19, 1955). RCP.

Letter from PB to MR (March 10, 1953). RCP.

Letter from BH to PB (October 10, 1955). RCP.

Letter from RC to Katherine Bernard (November 6, 1955). RCP.

Letter from BH to RC (August 10, 1956). RCP. Known today as "The Father of the National Wildlife Refuge System," J. Clark Salyer (1902–1966) began his career managing refuges for the former Bureau of Biological Survey. At the time of this letter, Salyer was chief of refuge management for the FWS. In honor of his dedication to the National Wildlife Refuge system, the Service renamed the Lower Souris NWR in North Dakota after Salyer in 1966.

Letter from RC to BH (August 2, 1963). Original in author's possession.

Letter from Yale University Library to BH (December 15, 1965). Original letter of acknowledgement in author's possession.

Letter from BH to Dorothy Freeman (Undated, circa 1969). Dorothy Freeman Collection, Edmund S. Muskie Archives and Special Collections, Bates College.

Letter from BH to RC (Undated). RCP.

Memo from Lovell Thompson (LT) to PB (June 11, 1951). RCP.

Memo from LT to PB (July 8, 1952). RCP.

BH/PA OH. Tapes 1–4 and 11–20. Paul Brooks chose the husband and wife team of Lois and Louis Darling to illustrate *Silent Spring*. During Hines's oral history, Hines revealed that Rachel Carson telephoned him and apologized. "Rachel actually called me up and cried over the phone. She was disappointed. It wasn't that [the Darlings'] drawings were so bad, it's just that she knew that I could have used the money. [A percentage] of the sales of *Silent Spring* would have fixed me pretty nicely." This recollection is apocryphal as there is no documentation that either Brooks or Carson considered Hines to illustrate the book.

Transcript of Interview with Bob Hines. April 25, 1991. Peace River Films Collection, Linda Lear Center for Special Collections & Archives, Connecticut College, New London, CT. Dr. Lear kindly shared a copy of her interview with Hines.

The five *Conservation in Action* titles and release dates that Hines illustrated are *Wheeler*, 1949; *Bear River*, 1950; *Red Rock Lakes*, 1953; *Stillwater*, 1953; and *Aransas*, 1954. The *Bear River* monograph has a stated price of ten cents; the others were fifteen cents apiece.

Chapter 8

Duncan, Dayton, and Burns, K., *The National Parks: America's Best Idea* (New York: Alfred A. Knopf, 2009).

Kalmbach, E. R., "Wildlife in the Mails," *Nature Magazine* (June–July 1950). Reprint in Hines's files.

Neel, Samuel E., "Proposal for a Series of United States Commemorative Stamps Honoring Wildlife Resources" (September 8, 1955). Copy in Hines's files.

Rueth, Carl P., "Antelope Best Design of 1956," *Linn's Weekly Stamp News* volume 30, number 2 (March 18, 1957): 1 and 7.

——, "U.S. Flag Best Design of 1957," *Linn's Weekly Stamp News* volume 31, number 2 (March 17, 1958): 11 and 4.

Scott, L. E., "Best Designs of 1958," *Stamp Collectors' Annual 1959* (London: Harris Publications, 1959): 37–41.

"U.S. Official Is to Direct Stamp Issue," *Fond du Lac Commonwealth Reporter* (May 2, 1956): 2.

"City Residents Given Awards for Top Displays of Stamps," *Fond du Lac Commonwealth Reporter* (May 3, 1956): 3.

"Collectors Swamp Local Postoffice [sic] for First Pronghorn Antelope Stamps," *The Courier* volume 29, number 22 (June 10, 1956): 1.

"Ceremonies commemorating the new Pronghorn Antelope stamp were held in front of Webster Hall Friday afternoon before a discouragingly small crowd," [caption] *Gunniston News-Champion* volume 56, number 5 (June 20, 1956).

"It's a Big Day at Postoffice [sic] for Collectors," *Seattle Daily Times* (November 9, 1956): 11.

"Removing treble hook lure from the back of my head. Yellowstone Lake, 1956." Original photograph with handwritten caption in author's possession.

"Notes Regarding Wildlife Conservation Postage Stamp Series" (October 2, 1957). Carbon copy in Hines's files.

"N.Y. Stamp Show Plans," *The New York Times* (November 18, 1957).

"The World of Stamps," *The New York Times* (December 8, 1957).

"Wildlife Species Nominated as Subjects for United States Commemorative Stamps Honoring Wildlife Resources." Undated document fragment, carbon copy in Hines's files.

"A History of Gunnison Postmasters." Undated newspaper clipping courtesy of Gunnison County Public Library.

Letter from Postmaster General to J. A. Krug (February 23, 1949). Copy in Hines's files.

Letter from E. R. Kalmbach to Olin Johnston (February 25, 1949). Carbon copy in Hines's files. Addendum: In 1937, President Franklin Roosevelt signed the Pittman Robertson Act into law. A federal excise tax on guns and ammunition provides funding for distribution to individual states.

Letter from Postmaster General to Eugene Millikin (February 25, 1949). Copy in Hines's files.

Letter from E. R. Kalmbach to BH (December 14, 1953). Original in Hines's files.

Letter from Samuel Neel to Aksel Nielsen (September 9, 1955). Dwight D. Eisenhower Presidential Library, National Archives and Record Administration (DEPL, NARA).

Letter from President Eisenhower to the Honorable Arthur E. Summerfield (September 15, 1955). DEPL, NARA.

Letter from Arthur Summerfield to President Eisenhower (September 29, 1955). DEPL, NARA.

Letter from Aksel Nielsen to Samuel Neel (September 29, 1955). Copy in Hines's files.

Letter from Aksel Nielsen to Samuel E. Neel (December 8, 1955). Original letter in Hines's files.

Letter from Thomas L. Kimball to the Honorable Dwight D. Eisenhower (February 24, 1956). DEPL, NARA.

Letter from BH to William S. Baunach (March 20, 1956). Carbon copy in Hines's files.

Letter from BH to RC (August 19, 1956). RCP.

Letter from John L. Farley to Robert W. Hines (October 8, 1956). Robert Hines Federal Personnel File, NPRC, NARA.

Letter from BH to RC (Undated, circa 1956). RCP. Hines wrote the letter regarding some questions with the German translation of *The Edge of the Sea*.

Memo from Jack Culbreath to Abram Tunison (August 1, 1957). Carbon copy in Hines's files.

Hines maintained that President Eisenhower instructed FBI Director J. Edgar Hoover to search for the stolen paintings. However, after multiple inquiries under the Freedom of Information Act, there appears to be no documentation of an FBI investigation. BH/PA OH. Tapes 13–16. Also, Pat Most, "Portrait of an Artist." Undated typescript copy in Hines's files [circa 1985].

Tom Duncan told the author about his time with Hines in Seattle in repeated conversations. Bob personally signed a sheet of the salmon stamps for Tom while they were together in Seattle. Mr. Duncan, a retired fisheries biologist with the FWS, inspired the author to tackle this biography of Hines.

Chapter 9

Austin, Elizabeth, "Recent Literature," *Bird-Banding* volume XXXVIII (April 1967): 167–69.

——, "Reviews," *The Auk* volume 88, number 1 (January 1971): 201.

Austin, O. L., "Recent Literature," *Bird-Banding* volume XXIII (July 1952): 135.

Linduska, Joseph (ed.), *Waterfowl Tomorrow*. (Washington, DC: U.S. Department of the Interior, BSFW, Government Printing Office, 1964).

Mann, William, "The Wild Animals in My Life," *National Geographic* (April 1957): 497–524. Nancy Miller's photograph appears on page 515.

Miller, Don, "Book on Fishing a Great Catch," *Chronicle-Telegram* (September 5, 1971): 15.

Saults, Dan, "Outdoor Books," *Outdoors Unlimited* volume 40, number 10 (October 1979): 22.

Stefferud, Alfred (ed.), *Birds in Our Lives* (Washington, DC: U.S. Department of the Interior, BSFW, Government Printing Office, 1966).

"Mrs. Robert W. Hines," *Fremont News Messenger* (December 9, 1965).

Certificate of Death. Edna D. Hines. December 8, 1965. Ohio Department of Health. Division of Vital Statistics.

"Bob Hines Completes a New Painting," *In-sight* (October 1968): 2.

"Interior Issues Some Basic Data on Duck Species Now in Short Supply" (September 4, 1958). Department of the Interior, Fish and Wildlife Service, Information Service (DOI/FWS, IS).

"Winter Waterfowl Survey, Other Data, Indicate Decline in Atlantic Duck Population" (September 15, 1958). DOI/FWS, IS.

"Hunters Urged to 'Look Harder' Before Shooting Ducks" (September 23, 1958). DOI/FWS, IS.

"Hunters Face Added Responsibilities in Coming Duck Season" (October 1, 1958). DOI/FWS, IS.

"Current Outlook for Waterfowl Production Considered Unpromising" (May 21, 1959). DOI/FWS, IS.

"Janzen Declares Duck Stamps Insurance for Future Duck Hunting" (June 9, 1959). DOI/FWS, IS.

"Breeding Ducks Caught Between Dust and Ice" (June 26, 1959). DOI/FWS, IS.

"Wildlife Official Summarizes Waterfowl Situation" (August 4, 1959). DOI/FWS, IS.

"Waterfowl Hunting Seasons to be Curtailed" (August 17, 1959). DOI/FWS, IS.

"Dates Announced for 1959–60 Waterfowl Hunting Season" (August 31, 1959). DOI/FWS, IS.

"Analysis Shows Heavy Hunter Effect on Canvasback Ducks" (September 13, 1959). DOI/FWS, IS.

"TV Shorts Tell Plight of Ducks, Give Tips to Hunters" (October 1, 1959). DOI/FWS, IS.

"Posters and Leaflet Part of FWS Waterfowl Education Program" (October 11, 1959). DOI/FWS, IS.

"Wildlife Official Supplies Chart for Duck Identification" (1959). DOI/FWS, IS (P.N. 62364-59).

"Duck Identification Leaflet Available, Wildlife Official Says" (1959). DOI/FWS, IS (P.N. 62365-59).

"Wildlife Official Urges Hunters to 'Let the Birds Come in Close'" (1959). DOI/FWS, IS (P.N. 62366-59).

"Radio Spots for Waterfowl Conservation" (1959). DOI/FWS, IS (P.N. 62367-59).

"Radio Spots for Waterfowl Conservation" (1959). DOI/FWS, IS (P.N. 62368-59).

"Winter Duck Count in Pacific Flyway Shows 18 Percent Decline" (February 12, 1960). DOI/FWS, IS.

"Bennett Opens Special Drive for Duck Stamp Sales" (February 20, 1960). DOI/FWS, IS.

"Nationwide Campaign Opens on Special Duck Stamp Sale." (March 4, 1960.) DOI/FWS, IS (P.N. 70379-60)

"Duck Flights Expected 'About Like Last Year' in Three Flyways: Down in Pacific" (August 9, 1960). DOI/FWS, IS.

"Hunting Restrictions Offer Chance to Reestablish Redhead and Canvasback Duck Flocks" (September 18, 1960). DOI/FWS, IS.

"Interior Department Asks Waterfowl Hunters to 'Know Their Ducks'" (September 18, 1963). FWS News Release.

"Interior's Waterfowl Guide Among 10 Top Government Best Sellers" (January 16, 1964). FWS News Release.

"New Waterfowl Volume Launched in Three-Nation Ceremony" (October 6, 1964). U.S. Department of the Interior News Release.

Certificate of Marriage. Commonwealth of Virginia. Robert Warren Hines and Nancy Hays Miller. July 22, 1966. Circuit Court of Arlington County. Clerk No. 1542.

"Bald Eagle Painting Reproduced by Department of the Interior" (August 28, 1966). BSFW News Release.

"Painting by Interior Employee New Department Publication," *IDRA News* volume 8, number 7–8 (September–October 1966): 1.

"Interior Department Publishes New Popular Volume on Birds" (October 8, 1966). Bureau of Sport Fisheries and Wildlife News Release.

"Distinguished Service Award" (June 7, 1971). Robert Hines Federal Personnel File, NPRC, NARA.

"Bird Watching for City Folk" (February 27, 1974). FWS News Release.

"Alaska's Rich Variety of Seabirds Profiled in New Wildlife Portrait Series" (January 2, 1980). FWS News Release.

"Mural Completed for Okefenokee Exhibit Room," Undated newspaper clipping [Folkston, Georgia]. Copy in Hines's files.

Letter from BH to PB (September 4, 1953). RCP. Hines suggested to Brooks that Houghton Mifflin Company might similarly reprint and distribute another FWS publication, "Alaska's Fish and Wildlife." However, Brooks declined, believing the topic was too geographically restricted to appeal to the general reading public.

Letter from Jay Darling to Philip DuMont (September 16, 1960). NPRC, NARA.

Letter from BH to Ferdinand Monjo (October 17, 1963). Peter Farb Collection. Western History and Genealogy. Denver (Colorado) Public Library.

Letter from Jack H. Berryman to Robert W. Hines (February 27, 1965). Robert Hines Federal Personnel file, NPRC, NARA.

Letter from BH to Dorothy Freeman (Undated, circa 1967). Dorothy Freeman Collection, Edmund S. Muskie Archives and Special Collections, Bates College.

Letter from Joseph Linduska to the American Motors Conservation Award Committee (November 27, 1970). Conservation Library, Denver Public Library. The committee did not present the award to Hines.

Letter from Barry Shillito to BH (September 16, 1971). Robert Hines Federal Personnel File, NPRC, NARA.

Letter from BH to Dorothy Freeman (Undated, circa 1977). Dorothy Freeman Collection, Edmund S. Muskie Archives, Bates College, Lewiston, Maine.

Letter from Robert C. Glotzhober to author (February 26, 2010).

Memo from Superintendent of National Capital Parks to Director of Office of Information, FWS (April 28, 1960). Robert Hines Federal Personnel File, NPRC, NARA.

Memo from R. W. Burwell to Clarence Pautzke (October 23, 1963). Robert Hines Federal Personnel File, NPRC, NARA.

Memo from John Mattoon (December 15, 1980). Robert Hines Federal Personnel File, NPRC, NARA.

BH/PA OH Tapes 1–4, 9–12, 13–16, 17–20, and 29–31.

There was friction between Hines and Bob Wells (1905–1962), the director of the Information Office who succeeded Alastair MacBain. In Hines's oral history, Hines refers to Wells with veiled sarcasm as "God's gift to ducks." A native of Upstate New York, Wells began his career as a newspaperman with the *Watertown Daily Times*. He spent two decades with the newspaper before he transitioned to the New York Conservation Department. Wells joined the FWS as an assistant to the director of the Service. He then became director of the Information Office in 1956 where he served in that capacity until his unexpected death at fifty-seven years of age.

"Know Your Ducks, Field Guide for Hunter." Copy in author's possession. See also "Interior launches drive to save canvasback and redhead ducks" (September 21, 1960). Department of the Interior, FWS, Information Service News Release.

There is no documentation regarding Hines in the Marie Rodell files, now the Frances Collin Literary Agency. Prior to her death in 1975, Rodell may have culled her files including material on Hines.

Nancy Hayes Miller, Federal Personnel File, NPRC, NARA.

Hon. Delbert L. Latta. Congressional Record (February 29, 1972).

Interview with NH (July 31, 2010).

Interview with Nancy Hines (July 31, 2010).

Interview with Pete Anastasi (January 24, 2010).

Interview with Clay Hardy (February 27, 2010).
Interview with Jo Keller (May 19, 2010).
Interview with Don Pfitzer (2010).
I thank Virginia and George Nunemacher of Columbus, Ohio, for sharing these family cards with me.
"George W. Hines" [obituary]. *Fremont News Messenger*. May 27, 1975.
Certificate of Death. George W. Hines. May 23, 1975. Commonwealth of Virginia. Department of Health, Division of Vital Records. Richmond.
The Blazed Trail, Abercrombie & Fitch Catalog (Spring 1975). According to the catalog, of the proceeds from the Don Crowley's National Fishing Stamp and print, "Trout Unlimited, The National Salmon Foundation, and The National Recreation and Park Association will receive respectively 5%, 5%, and 15% of the proceeds of its sale."
Parmelee, David, "Book Review: *Birds of the Antarctic and Subantarctic*," *The Wilson Bulletin* volume 89, number 4 (December 1977): 646–48.
The contract for *The Cats* stipulates $2,000 to Hines, "one half on receipt of this signed agreement and one half on acceptance of complete satisfactory artwork." Marie Rodell, "the artist's agent," would receive the payment and retain 10 percent as her fee.
African Safari Club Conservation Award recipients. Judge Russell Train received a Saudi Arabian oryx painting in 1967. Dr. Theodore Reed, veterinarian at the National Zoological Park, received a white tiger painting in 1969.

Chapter 10

Bruns, James, "Stamps and Coins," *The Washington Post* (January 2, 1983): K6. See also "Obituary: Beatrice Bialobreski," *The Washington Post* (December 19, 1982): B6.
Caldwell, William A. "Reflections of That Man Friday," *Vineyard Gazette* (February 13, 1981).
Causey, Mike, "The Federal Diary," *The Washington Post* (January 13, 1981): C2.
Gottschalk, John S., "Celebrating the Interior Department's Bob Hines Exhibit," Text of speech (February 23, 1994).
Hines, Bob, "Some Reminiscences on the Duck Stamp Contest," Undated typescript copy from Hines's files: 13.

Weiss, Michael J., "Bob Hines: A Wild Artist," *American Way* (May 1981): 104. *American Way* is the monthly periodical for American Airlines.

Letter BH to Tom Duncan (February 8, 1977). I thank Mr. Duncan for sharing this letter with me.

Letter from BH to Tom Duncan (June 20, 1985).

Letter from Truman M. Talley to BH (March 22, 1988). Copy in Hines's files. Truman Talley Books was a division of E. P. Dutton.

Excerpts come from Hines's retirement letters in the National Conservation Training Center Archives, Shepherdstown, West Virginia.

Memo from Jim Palmer to BH (February 26, 1991). Copy in Hines's files.

Memo from V. Daniel Stiles (December 5, 1994).

BH/PA OH Tapes 9–12, 17–20, and 29–31.

"National Duck Stamp Week. Golden Anniversary Year of the Duck Stamp, 1984" (July 3, 1984). Copy of presidential proclamation courtesy of the Ronald Reagan Presidential Library, Simi Valley, California.

Copy of raffle entry for the moose oil painting from Hines's files now in author's possession. The drawing for the raffle is dated October 2, 1983.

Christmas card from BH to Tom Duncan (1989).

"Separation and Property Settlement Agreement." Filed July 26, 1993. Circuit Court, Arlington, Virginia.

Certificate of Death. Robert W. Hines. November 6, 1994. Commonwealth of Virginia, Department of Health, Division of Vital Records, Richmond.

Interview with George Reiger (February 27, 2010).

Interview with Debra Berke (June 12, 2010).

Interview with NH (July 31, 2010).

Interview with Grayson Chesser (February 13, 2011).

Interview with Delbert "Cigar" Daisey (March 16, 2011).

An inquiry with Cherrydale Health Care Center (formerly Camelot Hall Nursing Home), Arlington, Virginia, reveals that the facility destroyed Hines's medical records after his death.

The exact site of Hines's final resting place is a family secret, remotely located in the southeastern corner of Ohio amongst Wayne National Forest.

Moose, Alaska's Animals and Fishes *(1946).*

Grayling, Alaska's Animals and Fishes *(1946).*

Caribou, Alaska's Animals and Fishes *(1946).*

Brown bear mural (1957).

Winter mallard duck mural (1957).

Autumn elks. Hines completed this painting for Interior Secretary Cecil Andrus. (1976).

Mattamuskeet mural. (circa 1950).

Brown trout. Hines wrote on the back of the canvas, "Duplicate of watercolor painted for President Eisenhower—and stolen from the White House—Denver 1955" (date unknown).

Beaver. National Wildlife Federation, "Conservation Stamp Album" (1957). Image courtesy of the National Conservation Training Center, USFWS.

"The Symbol of Our Nation" (USFWS, 1966).

Nighthawk, Fifty Birds of Town and City *(USFWS, 1975).*

Killdeer, Fifty Birds of Town and City *(USFWS, 1975).*

Steller's jay, "Wildlife Portraits No. 4" (USFWS, 1974).

Acorn woodpecker, "Wildlife Portraits No. 4" (USFWS, 1974).

Northern pike, Sport Fishing USA *(USFWS, 1971).*

Crappies, Sport Fishing USA *(USFWS, 1971).*

Pacific marlin, Sport Fishing USA *(USFWS, 1971)*.

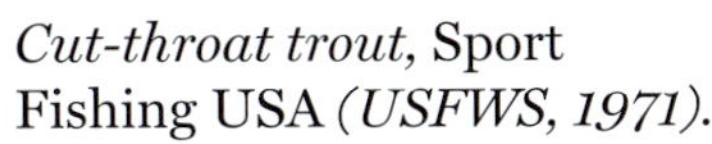

Cut-throat trout, Sport Fishing USA *(USFWS, 1971)*.

Cartoon for Interior Secretary Rogers C. B. Morton, (1971). Note the opposing factions present in wildlife conservation. Image courtesy of the Wendell H. Ford Research Center and Public Policy Archives, University of Kentucky.

Hines's winning design for the Abercrombie & Fitch National Fishing Stamp (1975).

High Arctic Summer, "A Host of Seabirds, Alaska" (USFWS, 1979).

Home Defense, "A Host of Seabirds, Alaska." (USFWS, 1979).

Murres, Alaskan porfolio (1979).

"Lightening Strike," Alaskan portfolio (1979).

"Salmon Fisherman," Alaskan portfolio (1979).

"Shenandoah Pride," First Virginia Wild Turkey Stamp (1982).

Hines prior to his retirement from the US Fish and Wildlife Service. Photograph by John Neubauer (1980). Used with permission from American Way.

Above: Young Bob Hines with friend (date unknown).
Below: Robert W. Hines, boyhood photograph (date unknown) courtesy of Mr. and Mrs. George Nunemacher.

Mabel Nunemacher Hines, Bob's beloved mother (date unknown). Photograph courtesy of Mr. and Mrs. George Nunemacher.

Above: George Hines [center] with sons Bill [left] and Bob [right] (circa 1970).

Edna D. Beatty, 1934 Flastacowo *yearbook. Used with permission of Florida State University.*
Left: Bob and Nancy Hays Hines (date unknown).

Bob Hines. High school graduation (circa 1927), courtesy of Mr. and Mrs. George Nunemacher.

Staff artist, Ohio Division of Conservation and Natural Resources (circa 1940).

Left: Pennsylvania Game News. (1943). This piece stands out from Hines's oeuvre because of its rare political statement.
Below: Early dog drawing (circa 1934).

Two "Under Ohio Skies" panels. Above: 11/29/43, Below: 11/1/43. Used with permission of the Ohio Department of Natural Resources.

An everyman for outdoors Ohio with Sally, his setter (1941).

Top: Hines's 1946 Federal Duck Stamp design. Right: Hines's shoveller duck design submitted for the 1945 Federal Duck Stamp.

Designer of the 1946 Federal Duck Stamp.

Left: Frank Dufresne (date unknown). Below: Hines fly fishing on Lake Wilson, Alaska (1947).

Above: Ermine scratchboard, the first piece of artwork that Hines completed as artist for the US Fish and Wildlife Service (1948). Below: After Hines observed a running wolf during his 1949 Manitoba trip, he described the canine in motion as "the most magnificent display of animal strength I have ever seen" (date unknown).

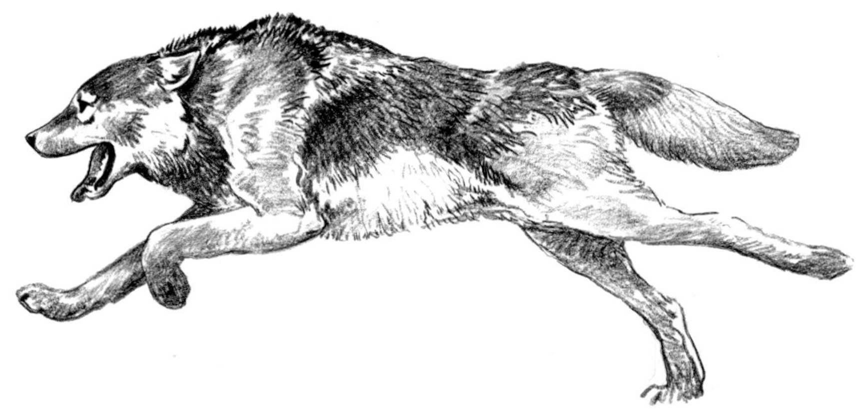

Fish and Wildlife Service Director Al Day [left] and Texas Congressman Clark W. Thompson [right] hold Walter Weber's trumpeter swan design, winner of the first open competition for the Federal Duck Stamp (1949).

Hines's retirement collage for Albert Day (1955).

Hines aside his commercial tuna fishing mural (1957).

Hines with his mallard duck mural (1957).

Hines painting his Mattamuskeet mural (early 1950s, USFWS).

Hines and Rachel Carson in the Florida Keys (1952, USFWS).

Top: Illustrator of The Edge of the Sea *(1955). Photograph courtesy of the Beinecke Rare Book and Manuscript Library, Yale University. Left: Jellyfish drawing from* The Edge of the Sea *(1955). Used with permission from Houghton Mifflin Harcourt. Above: Hines's ill-fated book plate design for* The Edge of the Sea *(1955). Image courtesy of the Beinecke Rare Book and Manuscript Library, Yale University.*

Above: Hines's photograph of Rachel Carson at her Maine cottage (1961). Right: Hines's undated pencil portrait of Carson

Gyrfalcon study, Alaska (1954).

Raven and magpie study, Alaska (1954).

Left: Hines bags his first emperor goose, Alaska (1954). Below: Three Federal Duck Stamp artists: [from left to right] Bob Hines, Ed Birely, and Walter Weber (1957).

Right: Hines paints his brown bear mural (1957). Below: Hines scuba diving for the Service (date unknown).

Hines with his whooping crane design for the wildlife conservation postage stamp (1957).

Hines's design for the 1956 wild turkey wildlife conservation postage stamp.

Hines and Jewett Hall, searching for alligators in Okeefenokee National Wildlife Refuge (1950s, USFWS).

A young admirer inspects Hines's Chesser Island mural in progress. Note the Carolina parakeets in the lower right hand corner that Hines inexplicably painted over. Photograph courtesy of Don Pfitzer. (1968)

Portrait of Hines, illustrator of Birds in Our Lives *(1966).*

Interior Secretary Stewart Udall with Hines. Bob is signing "The Symbol of Our Nation" print (1966).

Photographer Don Pfitzer captures one of Hines's power naps (1966).

Above: Interior Secretary Rogers C. B. Morton presents Hines the Citation for Distinguished Service (1971). Below: Hines with his Steller's jay painting (1974).